Praise for *The Mystery of Art*

With the lyrical immediacy that narrates his own path as a Christian and an artist, Jonathan Jackson draws on both his own experience and the richness of the theological tradition of the Orthodox Church to present not only intelligent thinking on aesthetics nor his contemplations on spiritual matters, but a fresh and genuine spiritual path for all artists and indeed for all persons. A delight to read, this book is not merely written—it sings.

—Fr. Andrew Stephen Damick,
Author of *Orthodoxy and Heterodoxy* and *An Introduction to God*

It is a delight to see Jonathan Jackson's book on Christianity and art being published by Ancient Faith. Not only does it address a question of perennial and—in our times especially—pressing interest, but does so with remarkable clarity and grace. Jonathan is a well-known actor, musician, and poet, and this inspired effort to bring the insights of his Orthodox Christian faith to all forms of artistic creativity can only be welcomed as an exciting event in the intellectual history of the modern Church.

—Fr. John Strickland, Author of *The Making of Holy Russia*

I was inspired by *The Mystery of Art*. Jonathan Jackson's approach to the role of an artist is holistic and challenging. He portrays the artist as a coworker with God, fashioned in His image. Throughout the book, Jonathan encourages us not only to uplift the culture, but also suffer for its renewal, with humility and love. As an artist, I was moved to contemplate the prayerful nature of each moment of creation.

—Michael W. Smith, Singer/Songwriter

The Mystery of Art

Becoming an Artist in the Image of God

JONATHAN JACKSON

ANCIENT FAITH PUBLISHING
CHESTERTON, INDIANA

Scripture quotations are taken from the New King James Version,
© 1979, 1980, 1982 by Thomas Nelson, Inc. Used by permission.

Published by:
    Ancient Faith Publishing
    A Division of Ancient Faith Ministries
    P.O. Box 748
    Chesterton, IN 46304

ISBN: 978-1-936270-32-3

Printed in the United States of America

Cover design by Bruce Petersen
Cover photo by Laura Godwin

For Elisa and Anthony

Contents

Foreword

Jonathan Jackson's effort is important not only for what he writes, but also because he wrote it. Many Orthodox Christians participate at the highest levels in the arts in the United States. But this is the first time a professional artist who is also Orthodox has described the relationship between his personal theology and his work. It is a sign, not only of Jonathan's devotion, but also of the maturation and participation of Orthodox Christianity in the broader intellectual and spiritual life of America, which is completely consistent with the cosmopolitan character of the Orthodox Christianity of Byzantium so long neglected in Western Europe and the Americas.

Maturity and participation are important themes for any endeavor, but particularly for the creation of art, irrespective of the precise kind of art. Maturity flowing from self-knowledge marks the work of the great artists. But maturity is not enough. Participation between the artist and his Creator, materials, and audience is an essential part of what allows artists to reach out to others across time and culture—to participate in the lives of other people and cultures long after death. So art is judged as more or less successful by its ability to reach others. As Christians we will be judged the same way. Do we use our faith to include, to welcome, and even to enjoy others? Every Christian must be part artist. We craft lives of meaning through faith. And this means reaching out to engage those who differ while never losing an appreciation for what sets us apart.

Participation also means acquiring wisdom to select the material proper to the end. We would not naturally make a Byzantine cross from New England granite or a Celtic cross from Italian marble. Actors don't laugh at television funerals unless there is a good reason. Just as we must inhabit the various responsibilities our relationships impose upon us, be they wife or husband or child or friend, actors must inhabit their characters "as with a garment," musicians must swim inside their own music and authors their prose. Sculptors and painters inhabit their work by relating to it intuitively—Michelangelo released David from the block of marble. And as Elder Joseph of Vatopaidi once said, "Our intuition is a glimmer of how Adam and Eve knew the world before the Fall." Mr. Jackson rightfully points out that performing artists, whether actors or musicians, use themselves as their material. This chameleon-like existence is full of pitfalls for personal identity and relationships. It is never more important to have a relationship with God, particularly Jesus Christ, because each time we engage art, each time we create, we participate in the Incarnation, which is just another way of inhabiting.

What does all this mean? Just that if we want to portray real things, then we must engage in real relationships: first with God and then with others. We must be present in our relationships, inhabit them, dwell in our purpose, and then reach out through our art and forge new Christ-filled relationships with others. And this is a very different kind of art from the escapism we often see today—this book is a first step in correcting that.

—Father Andrew of Athos, 8 October 2014

Whoever wants to become a Christian,
must first become a poet.

—SAINT PORPHYRIOS[1]

The Prayer of Art

The highest form of art is prayer: whether in the shape of a monologue, a soliloquy, or a stare: in the key of laughter or despair. Has it not fallen upon us to become living parables of life and death? Is it just a job, a paycheck, or a one-night stand with fame? Or is it cosmic, redemptive, and spiritually ordained? Is it simply pretend? Or is the fiction breathing life into reality, like a trusted friend, manifesting not only the motive of the means but also the consequence of the ends?

Is it merely the momentary entertainment of laughter and tears? Or is it, somehow mysteriously, enlightening our forgotten years, our present dreams and our future fears? Like Shakespeare and the Scriptures of old, are we not revealing the vanity of revenge and the sorrow of a love grown cold? Are we not projecting into the very hearts of our beloved audience the bliss of a sacred romance, the hope of restoration, and the grace of a second chance?

Have we not been fashioned in the image of the Trinity? We speak and so hope that some will hear it—knowing that the true artist within must be the Holy Spirit. For Christ is all and in all, and we encounter Him within each other—in the eyes of a sister or the wisdom of a mother, in the tears of a father or the embrace of a brother.

Rejoice, O artists, for you have all entertained angels unseen! How blessed are we to be children who believe, by vocation and—is it too dramatic to say—by destiny?

The first demand any work of any art makes upon us is surrender. Look. Listen. Receive. Get yourself out of the way. (There is no good asking first whether the work before you deserves such a surrender, for until you have surrendered you cannot possibly find out.)

C. S. LEWIS[2]

Introduction

One does not need to be a Christian to be a great artist. One does not need to be a Christian to paint beautifully, sing with conviction, write harrowing stories, or perform scenes with transcendent power. I have no intention of suggesting anything contrary to this. But is the life of the Christian antithetical or complementary to the vocation of an artist? Are they hostile to one another or deeply connected? The purpose of this book is to open a dialogue between the Christian soul and the mystery of art.

As an artist, I found it inspiring to research the history of Christianity and discover the intimate relationship between Christ and the arts. Through iconography, majestic cathedrals, and poetic hymnography, the Christian faithful of antiquity experienced Christ by means of a holistic, sacramental, and artistic reality. This early Christian vision did not divide the sacred from the secular or the physical from the spiritual, creating the schizophrenia of our modern religious psychology. The early centuries of Christianity reveal a Church that was a stranger to these dualistic notions. The "either/or" mentality was rejected over and over again in favor of mystery and paradox. The Church embraced a "both/and" revelation of God. Christians proclaim that Christ is both God and man. A complete paradox!

The mystery of the Incarnation of God is the very reason the Church uses icons and artistic symbols. Jesus Christ became flesh and blood: God made Himself visible to humanity. He became one of us so we could become one with Him and taste immortality. This is the very essence of Christian hope. Depicting the Image of Christ is an act of faith proclaiming the Incarnation. Alexander Schmemann wrote, "All icons are in essence icons of the incarnation."[3] The Gospels do not prevent artistic and symbolic expression—they are symbol, art, and reason all at once as the Divine Word. Gospel is both book and icon, inviting us into an encounter with God. "[Christ] is the image of the invisible God" (Col. 1:15). The word *image* has the same meaning as the word *icon*. This reality shapes the entire framework of this book.

Christian art is found all along the walls of the catacombs and the earliest house churches. Mystery and liturgical art were the means by which Christians communed with God. In the mind of the Apostles and the Fathers of the Church, Christ came to sanctify the whole world, which included the arts. Within this original Christian vision, the work of an artist was not seen as antithetical to the Christian vocation.

Fundamentalist expressions of Christianity did not exist in the early centuries of the Church, except in fringe cults. The result of various puritanical sects gaining momentum over the last few hundred years, particularly in the West, is a spiritual and psychological trauma in the Christian's relationship to the arts. This not only produces bad art, it hinders many great artists from embracing Christianity. Why would an artist embrace a religion that teaches him to be suspicious of beauty? From this perspective, all values, aspirations, aesthetic beauty, and emotional honesty are set aside. Art is reduced to its message. It is far from Dostoevsky's saying, "Beauty will save the world."[4]

In Christian mysticism, the artist assists in creating beauty. Works of art—films, songs, poems, or paintings—all bring the human heart and mind into an experience with Jesus Christ's Incarnation. "In the beginning was the Word" (John 1:1), *Logos*, which means *meaning, significance, wisdom*. Whenever an artist brings someone into the presence of meaning, in that moment his work becomes incarnational instead of ideological. The artist is salt and light; he awakens the heart to a deeper significance. Meaning is all around us. Significance rests in creation. Beauty subsists in the eternal present. We are meant to bring light, the light of the Transfiguration of Christ.

It is an incredible thing to discover that Christianity is an experience of saying *yes* to what is truly beautiful. The puritanical, legalistic, and fundamentalist strains of modern Christianity have left our culture traumatized by a Divinity that is not beautiful. But from the beginning, the pure ancient faith of Christ, which is still alive today, proclaims that God is beautiful! Creation is filled with His glory, and He loves the world so much He died to restore her beauty.

The original vision of Christianity was maintained in the East and faithfully passed on from generation to generation. There were no crusades or inquisitions, no papal demands for supremacy, no systematic theology or Reformation. This continuity allowed the pristine expression and original communion of the Faith to be upheld and to endure. Artists can be inspired by their mystical, sacramental, and artistic past. Perhaps it will confirm what many have known in their hearts and believed in a subconscious fashion: Christ and the arts are destined for each other.

I made the journey to the Christian East and found a home there, as a Christian and as an artist. The life of Christ is profoundly rich in meaning for the vocation of an artist. In this work, my prayer is that the artist will become more Christian and the Christian more artistic. These realities are not opposed to one another. It is a mystery worth contemplating: becoming an artist in the image of God.

The Unknowing

I am a mystery to myself, ever breathing, like the sea; caught in the rapture of flowing blood and blinking eyes. I seek with need the sun to shadow, every drop of rain released from a storm. What is needed is given freely in calming strings and violent ransom. You bring with Your presence the gift of transformation and the wonder of an amnesty without shame. "Peace," You whisper, "does not come to light from knowing, but from being known."

I had nothing to do with my flesh and spirit's arrival; my first breath was drawn without my consent. How could I, molded clay and author of nothing, know so great a thing? Could Romeo know what William's hand might wield? And though, more free than this, my plight or joy still remains: the surrender of self to the mystery of God, and the wonder of His knowing.

1

ART AS

Beauty

Beauty is mysterious as well as terrible.
God and the devil are fighting there,
and the battlefield is the heart of man.

FYODOR DOSTOEVSKY[5]

G od is the ultimate Artist and Poet. Being fashioned in His image means that we are also artists and poets, regardless of our vocation in life. We are artists in the way we love. We are poets in the way we pray. Everyone is an artist. We are cosmically bound to one another through a divine tapestry stretching across the ages. Each one of us has a unique part to play in the symphony of God's creation.

The most important work of an artist is not what he or she creates. It is in the work of being created by the grace of God.

The primary focus of the artist is the working out of his salvation. What the artist creates or produces in terms of works of art is always secondary to *becoming* a work of art in reality. The spiritual artist continually repents his ambition and *becomes* the poem. This happens by sitting at the feet of the Master and beholding His glory, as the woman Mary did. The artist does not merely write or sing songs—he becomes the song. He does not simply paint on a canvas; he himself becomes a painting for the glory of God. This is a very different vision of an artist from what our culture celebrates.

Our culture says the goal of the artist is fame, recognition, and worldly glory—to receive the applause of men. Jesus Christ, who is the Image of God and of true humanity, gives an entirely different vision. He says, "Do not let your left hand know what your right hand is doing" (Matt. 6:3). In essence, He says to the artist, "Let your light shine so the world may see your good works and praise your Father who is in heaven. But as far as you are concerned, do not receive glory from people. Do these things in secret. Retreat into the closet of your heart, where ceaseless prayer resides. Remain hidden and innocent of all conceit. Your Father who sees in secret will reward you in the open."

The fallen artist pines for human applause. The spiritual artist groans for secret communion with the Creator. He knows this only happens through *kenosis*, or self-emptying. Our society says the ultimate artistic virtues are entertainment, money, and fame. In this view, the artist is a means to a materialistic end: profit and power. In contrast to this, the ultimate virtues of the spiritual artist are sanctification and transformation. In a grace-infused worldview, the artist is more than a means to such heavenly ends; he participates in the world's redemption.

BEAUTY WILL SAVE THE WORLD

The poetry of the Akathist Hymn, "Glory to God for All Things," found in the effects of Protopresbyter Gregory Petrov after his death in a Soviet prison camp in 1940, expresses the mystery of the artist: In the wondrous blending of sounds it is Your call we hear; in the harmony of many voices, in the sublime beauty of music, in the glory of the works of great composers: You lead us to the threshold of paradise to come and to the choirs of angels. All true beauty has the power to draw the soul toward You and to make it sing in ecstasy: Alleluia!

Ikos 7
The breath of Your Holy Spirit inspires artists, poets, and scientists. The power of Your supreme knowledge makes them prophets and interpreters of Your laws, who reveal the depths of Your creative wisdom. Their works speak unwittingly of You. How great are You in Your creation! How great are You in man![6]

"All true beauty has the power to draw the soul toward You and to make it sing in ecstasy: Alleluia!" Dostoevsky would agree. In his brilliant novel *The Idiot*, Prince Myshkin believes the world will be saved by beauty. For him Christianity is that beauty. This is the vision of the spiritual artist.

CREATING A CULTURE

Damon of Athens said, "When modes of music change, the fundamental laws of the State always change with them."[7] Artists cultivate our culture. Politicians can write as many laws as they wish, but they will never change the heart of the culture. This belongs to the artists—and we do battle in the heart for the soul of society.

Our culture often produces dehumanizing art, which promotes the desensitization and alienation of our young. If we as a society continue to applaud artists who produce unreasonably violent, gory, or pornographic music and films, we should not be surprised when we see the desecration of our culture.

It is not a matter of free speech. It is a matter of conscience. The fact that the artist is free to produce such content does not mean it is praiseworthy. The artist has an incredible influence on the zeitgeist of our culture. An artist is one of the caretakers of the spiritual health of humanity. Producing films in which pornography is depicted in a comedic manner or in which the systematic slaughter of innocent people is glorified changes the culture.

The artist is placed within this cultural dynamic to bring about the return of the prodigal world to the beauty of life. The artist is not a prude or a fundamentalist—he is not afraid to show the depths of darkness or the honesty of life. But when he is called to portray the ugliness of humanity, he will not glorify it. He will not call it beautiful or praiseworthy. He will weep as he paints and tremble as he sings. The spiritual artist will pray for the life of the world as he portrays its desperate need for healing.

REORIENTING THE ARTIST

Beyond art itself, I am writing about who we are as human beings, as it relates to the image of the Eternal Artist. Our primary focus is on the mystical nature of art, not on practical details of craft, although some of these things will be touched upon. The intention is to reorient the artist toward his true home: the Kingdom of heaven. What is art? What is man? Who is God? How do these things interact? These are some of the questions that provide a framework for this book.

My life in the arts began when I was eleven. I have maintained a career in Hollywood ever since: working in film, television, the stage, music, writing, and directing. But I am not any one of these things. I am not an actor, although I act. I am not a musician, although I sing. I am not a writer, although I'm writing. I am not what I do. Who I am is a broken man embraced by a loving God.

My love for each of these artistic expressions is immense. I also love the people in these vocations. Many artists have enriched and transformed my life. Creative and spiritual interaction with my mad coworkers moves my heart. They inspire and challenge me on a daily basis. Many artists who do not consciously share these convictions still possess a grace and participation in the truths of traditional Christianity. Christ is "all and in all" (Col. 3:11).

BEAUTY AND SYNERGY

The first time my brother Richard played the drums while I jammed on the guitar was unforgettable. I was eleven. He was fourteen. I had been playing guitar for three years. He had played drums since he was seven. We had never played together. We had a basement with a drum set, and I brought my guitar down there and plugged it into a cheap amplifier.

The next half-hour astonished us. The noise! The adrenaline! The energy! The music! It was actual music! It was as if our basement ceiling opened up and the sun radiated upon us. We stared at each other, utterly amazed—did that just happen? Is that even possible?

Objectively the quality of our playing was probably not impressive. To us it was magnificent. Something shifted within us that day. Twenty years later, we're still playing music together and dreaming of how to create powerful and moving songs to share with people. A creative encounter happened in that basement. My instrument encountered his instrument, and something profound took place. It was the power of synergy. I loved playing the guitar, but it was nothing compared to playing the guitar while Richard hammered away on those drums. That was tremendous. That was the beginning of something: a flame not easy to douse.

Why are these moments so powerful? Perhaps because humanity is stumbling into something beautiful: a mystery in our nature. Creating is the art of encountering the beauty of life. Humanity was created in the Image of God. What does this mean?

THE IMAGE IS PLURAL

In the beginning, God said, "Let *Us* make man in *Our* image, according to *Our* likeness" (Gen. 1:26, emphasis added). The Image of God is plural. Man and woman were created in the Divine Image of the Trinity, Father, Son, and Holy Spirit: a God who is love and communion. This has profound implications for the life of the artist.

To be made in the Image of the Father, Son, and Holy Spirit means to be created for communion. All authentic creativity comes from God, whether the artist is aware of it or not. Every step of the way, the Father, the Son, and the Holy Spirit are creatively active in the world. In that sense, creation is ongoing. The artist can glimpse the wonder of eternity here and now.

Before the world was made, communion (and a community of sorts) existed within the Trinity. The poet enters into this realm of existence, where his mind and heart abide in the love of God. He begins to think from the power and humility of Christ instead of his isolated and intellectual faculties. Truth is revealed by the grace of God and not attained by the efforts of man. The artist is never more himself than when his heart is united with the Holy Spirit; when he approaches his craft as a kind of symphony with God.

The Trinitarian God is a personal God of beauty and relationship. The Incarnation of the Son of God reveals to the artist the intimate way in which God has chosen to interact with the world. The Eternal Author has entered His own play, in the middle of the second act no less, when all hell has broken loose—and become the Hero who saves and redeems His precious creation. After all, who knows His characters better than the Author? He named them and created every nuance of their soul.

Obviously, the analogy breaks down when we consider the brilliant gift of free will, which fictional characters in a play do not possess. But when a person witnesses a play or a film, somehow he still believes those characters do in fact possess the freedom to make choices. Is this reality not the most powerful dynamic of life and story—the reality of choice?

Transforming the Atmosphere

When he creates, the artist seeks to transform the atmosphere. He seeks to affect the heart and infuse the mind with glimpses of beauty and darkness. Art is a form of transcendent communication. It is a reaching out from the depths of one's soul to engross the imagination and will of another. Art is always both a medium and a prophecy.

An actor knows, for instance, that listening is one of the most important elements of his craft. He practices the art of engaging with another person spontaneously. But if he is to act in the Spirit, he must also learn to listen to the Spirit's Voice. This is the same for any art form. The artist enters into his relationship with God, as well as his relationship with others, in order to transform the atmosphere. He engages with the Holy One as he engages with his fellow artists.

This also applies to artists who work alone: painters staring at a blank canvas or writers gazing at a blank page. They are not alone. The Spirit of God is within them and around them. The work is always synergistic. The prayers of the saints, the angels, and the Mother of God also surround the artist. Creating in the Spirit enables one always to live in expectancy and openness to the moment. The artist moves by the Spirit and with the Spirit. Knowledge can only assist his encounter; it cannot create it.

A beautiful Scripture conveys the artist's incredible reliance on God: "'Not by might nor by power, but by My Spirit,' says the Lord of hosts" (Zech. 4:6). This is one of the most useful prayers to pray when approaching any character, scene, song, or poem. The Holy Spirit moves like the wind. The artist's job is to remain present with his or her Creator. Self-reliance must be replaced by humble faith.

Christ said, "I am the vine, you *are* the branches. He who abides in Me, and I in him, bears much fruit; for without Me you can do nothing" (John 15:5). To truly create is to embrace cooperation with God: to become a coworker with the Holy

Spirit (1 Cor. 3:9). It is to encounter the Holy One, one's fellow Image-bearers, and one's authentic self. It is to encounter the unfolding mystery of the Trinity.

In the ancient Christian baptismal service, Christ is referred to as "the excellent Artist."[8] Like Vincent van Gogh, we stand in awe of the preeminent Artist and say, "[Christ] lived a serene life, *and was the greatest artist of all, disdaining marble, clay or colour, working with living flesh.* That is to say that this unbelievable artist, one who is scarcely conceivable to such an obtuse instrument as the modern neurotic, worn-out brain, made neither statues, nor pictures, nor books; indeed, he said clearly enough what he was doing—*fashioning living men*, immortal beings."[9]

THE SMALLEST GLIMPSE

These meditations can only provide a glimpse into these possibilities. But even the smallest glimpse, the most fleeting moment of spiritual union with the Beautiful One, is enough to break the soul's isolation and fear of abandonment and to awaken the immortal ache of the heart. The ancient Hebrew king expressed the paradoxical truth that God "put eternity in their hearts, except that no one can find out the work that God does from beginning to end" (Eccl. 3:11).

We possess these longings. We cannot deny them. We long for the transcendent voice, the eternal embrace, the personal cosmic rapture of our souls. Eternity itself is a dynamic state of transformation: an ever-deepening union with the Divine. It is not a static, impersonal state of having arrived once and for all. This is where we begin the journey, and where we shall return: in the tension of mystery and experience.

This is a prayer of fire hurled into the fearsome atmosphere of the human heart and mind. I pray these words lead to a holy silence: a silence that gives way to an encounter with the Author of your soul. May the Source of all creativity and love abide in the temple of your soul and bring you into the peace of His presence.

2

ART AS

Mystery &
Madness

*Before we define art or any concept, we must
answer a far broader question: what's the meaning
of man's life on Earth? Maybe we are here to enhance
ourselves spiritually: if our life tends to this spiritual
enrichment then art is a means to get there. This of
course, is in accordance with my definition of life.
Art should help man in this process. . . . Art enriches
man's own spiritual capabilities and he can then rise
above himself to use what we call 'free will.'*

ANDREI TARKOVSKY[10]

STARING INTO THE ABYSS

Anthony Geary is one of the best actors of his generation. He is a seven-time Emmy Award winner and has riveted audiences for decades with his heart-wrenching performances. He delves into the complexities of human suffering like a master craftsman. More than all of this, he is a true friend. At a very young age, I was placed under his tutelage. What a blessing! Not simply for me as an artist, but also as a human being. No one has meant more to my journey as an artist. Anthony once told me, "Sometimes right before I begin a scene, I imagine myself staring into the abyss."

What did he mean? It was poetic: I understood before I thought it through. I have shared this artistic reality with Anthony more times than I could recount. Over the course of many years, we portrayed an immensely tragic and loving relationship between a father and son. In the last storyline we performed together, the father had accidentally killed his grandson (his own son's son) while driving drunk. The anguish, guilt, shame, horror, fear, and regret were extreme. We walked through this together, both in tears, crying out at the injustice and absurdity of life. We stared into the abyss together. We trusted each other enough to do this. The synergy that took place was palpable. The atmosphere was changed—and so were we. The only word Anthony could use to describe it later was "transcendent."

This is a very Christian way of approaching art. You could

almost call it *apophatic art,* to use a highly theological phrase. We embrace what we don't know. Is the goal to acquire as much information as possible about acting, or songwriting, or painting? Is the goal solely to focus on what can be known and applied? Or is there more to it than this?

THE BREAD OF TECHNIQUE

In our time, art has been reduced almost to a science. The mystery of art is a memory. Actors and songwriters seek diverse methods of instruction as if someone could learn how to be an artist merely by learning a particular method or technique. Now, instruction in itself is not to be disparaged; but if these methods eclipse the mystery of art, then the artist has lost something. He has lost something essential about himself. He has divorced his craft from its spiritual roots. He has ceased to be the mystical being he is and become a modern rationalist. And yet the artist still yearns to be in the moment or emotionally available in his work. But there is another way for the artist to approach these ideals. Christ said, "Unless you are converted and become as little children, you will by no means enter the kingdom of heaven" (Matt. 18:3).

The words of Christ apply beautifully to artists. Little children learn by imitation and absorption. They are both humble and sensitive. Children live in the present moment. They are less concerned about themselves and more concerned with the action that is occurring. They laugh easily and cry without pretense. Their imaginations are alert and active. They feel before they think. They listen with their heart and their soul—their minds follow. Children always remain in a state of wonder and expectancy. A mundane thing to an adult can captivate a child's imagination for hours—how many times have we seen a child prefer the box to the toy?

Every art form has many different useful, even essential, techniques. But these techniques and methods must never replace one's innocence—or one's dependency on God as the true Creator.

When the devil tempted Christ in the wilderness, the Lord responded by saying, "It is written, 'Man shall not live by bread alone, but by every word that proceeds from the mouth of God'" (Matt. 4:4). This reveals that the artist relies on God more than on the technical aspects of his craft—the "bread" of technique and skill. Technique is very important, but flesh and bones without a spirit are dead. The Spirit of God whispers, "Listen."

Allowing technical methods to replace innocence, wonder, and dependency on the Holy Spirit is similar to allowing ritual to replace one's actual relationship with God. Do we rely on our religious methods and legalisms or on our intimacy and encounter with God? Do we rely on our technique as artists or on our openness to the Spirit of God? Are we prophets or performers? Are we icons of God or imposters?

Actors do not simply pretend: they reveal. Acting does not lie. It tells the truth in a parable. If acting were pretending, perhaps technique would suffice. But if acting is prophecy, then the actor needs God to help him perform truly, and God is present whether the artist is consciously aware of it or not.

ART CANNOT BE TAUGHT

Theology cannot be grasped intellectually. It can only be experienced. So it is with art. Ultimately, as someone once said, "art cannot be taught, it can only be caught." Many methods can be attached to the way of the Artist, but they will always remain subject to the mystery of communion with God. I hope that within these writings, God will capture your imagination, and what you discover will become truly alive. It will become more than abstraction, but a living experience. I am not disparaging technique—only attempting to place it within the majesty of the Eternal Artist.

Each human being has been called to a destiny that is both prophetic and artistic. The Son of God spoke in parables. The artist is called to become a living parable of hope, faith, love, sin, sorrow, despair, darkness, salvation, and grace. He portrays the radiance of God's love, laughter, joy, passion, and song. He will also enter into the depths of human frailty, mourning, and fear, in imitation of Christ.

In this prophetic way, the artist aligns himself with the sufferings of Christ and becomes a light for those who are bound in darkness. This power does not come to the self-assured or the hopelessly insecure. It belongs rather, to little children—to those who inherently embrace their weakness and yet possess an immutable confidence in the joy of learning.

Anthony Geary wrote me a letter, just as I was beginning to film *The Deep End of the Ocean*. In it he wrote, "You cannot act information." There is always plenty of information to assimilate—but it is just as important to embrace what cannot be understood or learned.

This places the artist on the appropriate mark, so to speak, and aligns him not only as a creator but also as a created person. Ultimately, that is what he is: part of the creation. He creates nothing himself, in any true or actual sense of the word. The artist discovers—through grace, inspiration, and osmosis with God and those he journeys with.

The artist can say, "This is what I have discovered, this is the information I have, but it is not enough—there is so much left, beyond my comprehension. I am still a child. I am still moving forward in discovery." This is why silence becomes such an important discipline. We will explore the theme of silence in a later chapter.

For now, we will shift our gaze from the theme of mystery to the theme of madness.

ART AS MADNESS

The most incredible artists and performers make you believe that at any moment, anything is possible. There is a transcendent quality to their work. Charlie Rose once asked Michael Stipe for the common thread among his artistic influences. His response was telling: "They have that same direct connection to the source. There's something flowing through them that is maybe bigger than the person . . . they're in a way a conduit to something much greater."[11]

It's soul-stirring and even transcendent to witness this kind of performance—as if the artist might break through the screen, jump down from the stage, come charging directly at the people, or vanish in some inexplicable way. Madness rivets the audience with its creative gift.

Sir Daniel Day-Lewis and Sir Anthony Hopkins are wonderful examples—the way their subdued rage suddenly explodes like a tidal wave. The subtlest look can evoke bottomless empathy. Comedians such as Robin Williams and Jim Carrey build their performances brilliantly, leaving audiences breathless from laughter. Meryl Streep's performances have myriad undercurrents that leave one truly mesmerized. Anything is possible within this place of artistic madness.

In the realm of music, think of the poetry of Leonard Cohen and Bob Dylan, or the live performances of the Doors, Jimmy Hendricks, Radiohead, U2, or R.E.M. Film? Think of directors like Fellini, Kubrick, Polanski, and Hitchcock.

Was Mozart normal? Was Beethoven balanced? Was Dostoevsky a respected citizen? Or were they mad on some level? Were they all outcasts to some degree? Was James Dean able to cope with life? Or did he wrestle with demons just beneath the surface? Didn't Van Gogh cut off his own ear? And on and on it goes.

Artists do not feel balanced or normal. Nobody becomes an actor, painter, writer, musician, or dancer to play it safe (or make a steady income). Most of our artistic heroes were and are self-destructive and deeply tormented. And so many have grown up believing that in order to be a brilliant artist, one must become tortured. If one already happens to be a lost soul, he must embrace it for the sake of his art—a sacrificial means to a glorious end. Our culture seems to believe that madness is a prerequisite for greatness, and so young artists accept this fate as their own—not just creatively, but personally.

This reality is partially true. I do, however, want to challenge the assumptions. I believe a kind of madness is required. But is madness inherently self-destructive? Or is it merely the manner in which the artist engages in the spiritual nature of his art?

Perhaps there are two kinds of madness. One is self-destructive, narcissistic, and tormented; the other therapeutic, selfless, and holy. One leads to loneliness and death, the other to wholeness and life. One leads to chaos; the other leads to sanity. Both can produce brilliant art (and this is where it gets tricky), but only one can produce both brilliant art and a brilliant life. Is it possible to render harrowing and earthshaking performances or write transformative songs without descending into turmoil and self-destruction? Could Dostoevsky write his dark themes and hold fast to the light? Dostoevsky was a lighthouse on my journey. He wrote about murder, madness, and salvation—all from an inner place of illumination.

Dostoevsky was a tortured soul in many ways. He endured a harrowing mock execution after being arrested for attending subversive political meetings. The experience haunted him the rest of his life. He suffered a lifelong battle with epilepsy in addition to imprisonment and the deaths of his first wife, brother, and two young children. He became a compulsive gambler, always struggling to pay off debts.

But somehow, Dostoevsky found a way to transform his suffering and give it meaning. The only way he could do this was through his faith in the suffering Christ. He glimpsed the madness of love. This glimpse inspired him to write some of the most profound literary works in history. In the darkness he found light. In death he witnessed the Risen Christ.

Contemplate the madness of the prophets and the saints. Some saints lived in the wilderness or on the tops of pillars for years on end. Some challenged kings and rulers. Moses was mad enough to repeatedly defy Pharaoh. Some prophets stood naked before crowds, hoping to awaken them to their own spiritual poverty. There is a whole category of saints known as "fools for Christ." Saint Simeon, the "feigner of idiocy," would skip, dance, and make up strange songs to reveal the truth to people. The Russian film *Ostrov (The Island)* is a powerful example of holy madness and the beauty of repentant prayer.[12]

This is not normal behavior!

In contemplating the crucified Christ, we discover the most extreme madness of all. Picture the most innocent man ever to live carrying the Cross of humanity's sins, and as God destroying death by death. Picture Him hanging naked before a mocking world. Can you even imagine the depth of love He must have possessed to suffer the Crucifixion? Is it possible to comprehend the defiant nature of His love as He cried out, "Forgive them, Father, for they know not what they do!" He was "staring into the abyss" for all of humanity. It is sheer madness on a cosmic scale!

What the artist learns from Christ is the madness of love: the extent to which the Divine will go to make us one with Him. In the eyes of the world, God's love is the highest form of insanity. The Scriptures declare, "God is Love" (1 John 4:16); this means that in some mysterious and sacred way, God is mad! Not in the sense that He is disturbed, but in the sense that His love reaches beyond the borders of convention and decency, right into the flaming heart of eternity.

To love like Christ is madness to the world. The world teaches that liberation is to love oneself above all. The humility of God is a scandal to the world. Monks of Mount Athos are madmen. Thank God for their prayers. Saint John Climacus wrote in *The Ladder of Divine Ascent* that love "does not fall, does not stop in its course, and allows no respite to him who is wounded by its blessed madness."[13]

Artists who desire to create in the Spirit are invited to encounter the Source of their originality. There is a depth of compassion in the heart of Christ that reaches beyond the temporal means of artistry—a voice crying out in the wilderness of your spirit!

It is a holy madness.

The True Artist is the Holy Spirit. He is the Eternal Poet, Master of story, Creator of light and motion, and Lord of life.

BECOMING A TRUE ICON

I would like to turn to another theme: the icon. What does it mean to become an icon? The world has many answers, some of which you already know. But I wish to offer another—one independent of box office sales, Academy Awards, Grammys, or tabloid arrests. This glory will last longer than fifteen minutes of fame or a lifetime of worldly praise. Truly, it abides in the realm of eternity.

The artist was created to be an icon of God, not a whore for the world to worship, ravage, and then discard. Not a self-god, but a child of God. For the artist, destiny and fame are not meant for the fleeting illusions of forgotten ages. Glory is not to be found in the vain applause of the hopelessly insecure. Worldly power is short-lived; like the grass, it is here today and gone tomorrow. Christ Himself enlightened the artists of the world when He said:

> "Do not lay up for yourselves treasures on earth, where moth
> and rust destroy and where thieves break in and steal; but lay
> up for yourselves treasures in heaven, where neither moth
> nor rust destroys and where thieves do not break in and steal.
> For where your treasure is, there your heart will be also."
> (Matt. 6:19–21)

The Greek word *eikon*, from which we get the English word *icon*, primarily means "image." We could say, "Man was created in the *icon* of God" (see Gen. 1:27). But it's an image damaged by conceit and self-rule. We have all become infected

with the sickness of sin, but the divine image of love nevertheless resides inside us. It must be restored to its original beauty
and innocence for it to live in the fullness of God.

Man is at once glorious and broken—magnificently radiant and deeply wounded. He is wounded, but not utterly
depraved. He cannot cease to yearn for immortality any more
than he can cease to hunger for food and water. "[God] has
put eternity into man's heart," the ancient Hebrew king proclaimed (Eccl. 3:11).

There is no escaping Hamlet's question, "To be or not to
be." It belongs to each one of us. The artist cannot escape asking the eternal questions. He must find a transcendent purpose for living. He must discover his madness and become a
martyr for something. But he has a choice. Will he create for
the glory of his small story or for the eternal glory of God?
Will his art be an offering for his own ego—or for the life of
the world?

Christ is the icon of both God and man. He is the Eternal
Image of God and the redeemed image of man. To behold
Christ is to glimpse the madness of heaven and to relinquish
all delusions of control. It is to become truly sane and mature.
It is to believe—to finally believe that in His presence, anything
is indeed possible.

To become a true icon means to be refashioned into His
Image and Likeness. Contrary to hypocritical religion, the art-
ist is not called merely to imitate Christ, but to become like
Him in his innermost being, by the grace of the Holy Spirit.
He is to think like Him and feel like Him. To see the way

Christ sees. To pray the way the Son prays. Love the way He loves. Create the way He creates. As Saint John Chrysostom said, "If artists who make statues and paint portraits of kings are held in high esteem, will not God bless ten thousand times more those who reveal and beautify His royal image (for man is the image of God)?"[14]

The artist is called not merely to imitate, but to become. Only then will his imitation be true and genuine, not hypocritical, self-righteous, and vain. Only then will his performances, poems, and songs become actions of love and transformation. Only then will his craft become transcendent and reflect something of eternal beauty and worth.

—⟢◆⟣—

A Prayer

O Spirit of Grace, you are complete and utter bliss. You are the ecstasy of a thousand kisses beneath the ocean. You are the rain of restoration and hope. You are the trembling inside my frame. You are the tears that have no end. You are the lightning of inspiration within my temple of wanderings. You are the heart of desire and the warmth of intimacy. You gave us your holy Law of Relationship in the mystery of your Embodiment. I yearn not for the hollow embrace of enlightenment, but for the holy embrace of your Person. My heart needs to be known more than to master knowledge.

If I gathered up all the fragments of enlightenment spread throughout the earth, I would still miss you, O God of intimacy. You alone have made yourself visible to my longing. You alone behold my humanity with affinity. Your heart touches my heart. Your eyes gaze upon my eyes. Your Spirit abides in my spirit. I reach out, and you reach back to me. I need you, and you choose to need me. O Rose of Sharon, my spirit trembles with expectancy. Wisdom is your presence. Salvation is your embrace. Heaven is to be seen by you. I fall into your arms of love. Through a blessed river of tears, I rest upon your gaze. I drink the revelation of your intent. I breathe the smoke of your radiance. I am here to be loved and to love you. I am here to be known and to know you. I am here to be seen and to see you. I am here to be embraced and to embrace you.

I trust not the systems of man. I need no Law save you, the Genesis of relationship. For you are written on the tablets of my heart and bound to the baileys of my reason. I worship no rituals or traditions save the sacrament of your love. I am bound to the ceremony of intimacy. I drink the wine of your presence every moment, in wilderness, prison, or temple. I eat the bread of your presence even while I sleep or converse with your sacred ones. I hear the sonnets of your devotion in the white of doves and the breeze of laughter. I behold the passion of your merciful dream—intimacy.[15]

3

ART AS

Prayer &
Intercession

They will keep the fabric of the world stable,
And their prayer is in the practice of their craft.

WISDOM OF SIRACH 38:34

Years ago, I worked with an actor I greatly admired, an Academy Award winner who had delivered countless soul-stirring performances. I was excited. Working with Anthony Geary for so many years had prepared me for the moment. It was an amazing experience. Something very powerful occurred, and it was a true joy to be a part of the creative process. However, the greatest joy was not the scenes themselves, but the simple act of prayer that occurred over the course of the work.

I ended up writing this person a note expressing that I saw him as an anointed artist, a man of God—and that I also believed one of the main reasons I got the job was to pray for him. I didn't know how he would react. I didn't know where his spiritual life was. But I knew I had to let him know that his work was about more than fame and recognition, that he was more than a great actor; he was known and loved by God and had been given a great gift.

The response was humbling and beautiful. He sought me out to thank me for the note. It meant something to him as an artist and as a person. It was a simple act of prayer and spiritual encouragement.

An artist's role transcends the art itself and includes the fullness of life—not only the fiction of what is being created, but also the reality of what is going on around her all the time. It is a holistic interior disposition of prayer and openness to God.

A LIFE OF CEASELESS PRAYER

The artist is called to embark on a life of ceaseless prayer (see 1 Thess. 5:17). This is what the Scriptures reveal. But what does this mean? How does this apply to the artist's life and craft? Here lies an ocean of possibilities. What does it mean to "pray without ceasing," as the Apostle Paul enjoined us to do? Ultimately, this is a revelation not of what the artist is to do, but what she is to become.

Christ cleared the Temple and said with unquenchable fire, "It is written, 'My house shall be called a house of prayer,' but you have made it a 'den of thieves'" (Matt. 21:13). His house shall be a house of prayer. St. Paul the Apostle wrote, "Do you not know that you are the temple of God and that the Spirit of God dwells in you?" (1 Cor. 3:16).

The artist is God's temple. She must become a "house of prayer." Christ must cleanse the artist, as He did Solomon's Temple, re-establishing the correct spiritual reality and the "right glory" within in her heart. It is an authenticity drenched in personal union with God. The artist's actions are merely manifestations of this inward reality.

The artist is to become a living prayer.

To pray means to interact. It means to engage with the intentions of the Holy One. Prayer is always relational, and so is art. It is a state of intimacy and wonder. To pray is to be in awe of God—to experience the mystery of everlasting love. The artist's performances and works of art are built from the inside out. At the deepest level, they cease to be performances or works of art as such and become seamless acts of prayer. In this way, the artist fulfills the directive to "pray without ceasing." The prayer of the heart, or the Jesus prayer—"Lord Jesus Christ, Son of God, have mercy on me, a sinner"—has been used for centuries by Orthodox monastics and laypeople, said continuously as a way of keeping the heart centered on God. It is an essential part of this mystery.

There is no separation between the sacred and the secular when one is living in communion with the Trinity. Father Alexander Schmemann proclaimed this in his seminal work, *For the Life of the World*:

> The world is a fallen world because it has fallen away from the awareness that God is all in all. The accumulation of this disregard for God is the original sin that blights the world. And even the religion of this fallen world cannot heal or redeem it, for it has accepted the reduction of God to an area called "sacred" ("spiritual," "supernatural")—as opposed to the world as "profane." It has accepted the all-embracing secularism which attempts to steal the world away from God.[16]

Paul Evdokimov expressed it this way: "There is no ontological dualism between the Church and the world, between the sacred and the profane. The only dualism is ethical, that of the 'new creation,' and the 'old man,' of the sacred (redeemed) and of the profane (demonized)."[17]

The role of the artist is to bridge this gap and fill the world with grace. Prayer is not relegated to church or to specific times of the day. The artist does not pray at the beginning and the end of the day; she prays always and everywhere, for everyone and everything. The stage or studio itself becomes sacred, because everything God made is for His glory. The blank page is a holy garden waiting to be cultivated by a son or daughter of God. The musical instrument is a spiritual weapon placed into the hands of a sacred vessel.

In Christ, everything man sees, touches, and encounters becomes transformed and redeemed. He seeks to unite, not to separate. He longs to heal, not to condemn. There is no such thing as sacred art or profane art in this context. The world becomes profane only when it is approached as a thing in and of itself. The grace of the Church should fill the Christian to overflowing, whereby she reenters the world carrying within her the mystery of Christ's love.

To the artist, this means that every song is a prayer. Every painting is a cry for transcendence and revelation. Every film is a parable of beauty or the emptiness of life without hope and meaning. We are all children drawing pictures to make sense of our pain. But we are also trying to make sense of the beauty we can't seem to shake, irrespective of life's ugliness. All of humanity is on its knees, every second of every day. Rebellion is a prayer; resignation is the desperate supplication for the end of disappointments. Laughter is the medicine of angels. Story is man's participation in the brilliance of God. On some level, we are all crying out, "My God, my God, why have You forsaken me?" (see Matt. 27:46). When Christ echoed this psalm on the Cross, He spoke for humanity.

It was a cosmic cry, wherein the cries of every man and woman from the beginning of time were lifted up to God at the perfect pitch of empathy, forgiveness, and grace. Life is prayer. Prayer is life.

From this place of inner communion with God, the artist

becomes (for the first time) truly open to others, both person-ally and cosmically. She also becomes open to herself and to God. As Stephen Muse wrote, "Prayer arises out of observing the human condition and looking to God for help and com-panionship."[18]

Prayer is the place of encounter between God, the world, and the self. *The Ladder of Divine Ascent* illumines the heart on the nature of prayer. In the inspired words of St. John Climacus:

> Prayer is the mother and daughter of tears. It is an expiation of sin, a bridge across temptation, a bulwark against afflic-tion. It wipes out conflict, is the work of angels, and is the nourishment of all bodiless beings. Prayer is future gladness, action without end, wellspring of virtues, source of grace, hidden progress, food of the soul, enlightenment of the mind, an axe against despair, hope demonstrated, sorrow done away with.[19]

Prayer is the artist's great reward. It is not an entitlement, but a gift. It is the gift of entering into communion with the Unap-proachable One, who made Himself accessible to humanity by the grace and Incarnation of His Son. The reward of prayer is listening to the wonders of God's love.

When a human being sacrifices in this life, her reward is not to be found in the material world, but in the secrecy of prayer. It is her reward not because she has earned it; it is her reward by grace, by virtue of her unique value to the Father of lights. The Cross of Christ and His Resurrection have won this reward for her. Prayer is the continual dwelling place of communion with the Trinity. It is the Source of the artist's joy and creativity, where she experiences the ecstasy of the Holy Spirit.

We will now expand to the realm of prayer as intercession, never losing the foundation of prayer as personal communion with God.

BUILDING TOWARD INTERCESSION: KARMA VS. GRACE

The ancient story of Job brings to the forefront one of the biggest questions of all: Why do we suffer? And even more to the point: Why do good people suffer? In the spirituality of our age, karma is the prevailing law of the universe. What a person puts out will ultimately come back to him, good or bad. The individual brought it upon himself. This law is supposed to motivate people to be good to each other; but it lacks an extremely important spiritual ingredient. What karma essentially means is that the individual is his own god. This is why it sells. It feels good at the outset to believe you are in control of your own destiny.

But what happens when tragedy strikes? What happens when a tornado hits? Is it your fault? Did you somehow bring this upon yourself? Did you do something horrible in a past life to warrant such devastation? Karma would mysteriously answer, *yes*. And if success comes your way, what can we conclude from this fortunate set of circumstances? The law of karma would say, "Congrats, it was all you!" The only spiritual endgame of this law is either pride or guilt. It might create a degree of behavior modification, but actual transformation of the soul requires something more.

Don't misunderstand; cause and effect exist. What you sow, you will reap. But the law of karma is not the ultimate law of the universe; it is only an axiom. The first law is grace. I'll explain this in more depth momentarily, but first we must walk through the problem of suffering if we hope to understand the meaning of grace. This can happen only in the presence of the Wounded God.

The Book of Job dramatically and comprehensively opposes any assumption of karma as an overriding law of creation. The character of Job foreshadows Christ: an innocent man experiencing the horrors of unmerited suffering. A truly righteous man, blameless in all his ways, in one tragedy after another Job loses everything: his children, his land, his crops. Finally he is left sitting in ashes with a terrible disease, bemoaning the day he was born.

Why has this happened?

Job's friends gather around him and muse about the reasons for his great suffering. "He must have done something to bring this upon himself," some of them suggest. "It must be karma for some unknown sin from his past! Things like this don't just happen. Right?"

But they do.

Horrible things happen to wonderful people—even to innocent children, who did nothing to deserve it. There are no easy answers or philosophical justifications to explain the problem of suffering. It is a mystery.

Job's story ends with an encounter with the Almighty that silences all our suppositions. There is no answer in this life. There is no "1+1=2" when it comes to suffering. There is a deep silence from the heavens—a silence each one of us will eventually encounter at some point in our lives, if we haven't already.

The shocking reality of Jesus Christ is that He entered into humanity's sorrow and agony completely: into the silence of God. By entering into this harrowing silence—by experiencing it on behalf of all—He broke the silence. The Eternal One, by assuming humanity's anguish and dying in the garment of our flesh on the Cross, completely changed the epicenter of our relationship to the mystery of suffering. God was not silent in the Incarnate Christ. He transformed suffering and gave it meaning.

The Son of God knows what it feels like to cry out, "My God, my God, why have You forsaken Me?" and receive only silence in response. The Innocent One took on the sins of the world. He did nothing to deserve crucifixion or the condemnation of others. Nevertheless, He suffered for the sake of our freedom and healing. This is not the law of karma—it is the law of grace.

It is this divine fountain that the artist draws from in order to portray the sufferings and joy of humanity. She shares in the suffering of Christ. She immerses herself in the compassionate love of God. She approaches the mystery of the Crucified One and calls upon the power of the Resurrection. This releases mercy and healing upon everyone who encounters what is being portrayed through her performances, songs, and works of art. How does the artist go about this sacred work?

ART AS INTERCESSION, EMPATHY, AND SACRIFICE

A quick story of intercession in the realm of acting: I was doing a scene on *General Hospital* where my character, Lucky, was given the news that his four-year-old son had just died: a tragedy beyond words. The whole set had a heaviness to it. Everyone could feel the intensity. No one wanted to portray this kind of storyline. It was brutal and horrifying to contemplate and enter into.

Part of my preparation for the scene was to pray for all those who had lost someone they loved, particularly parents who had lost their children. I wanted to make sure my heart was aligned with the compassion of Christ and open to the suffering of humanity. A sort of cosmic intercession was taking place. Meanwhile, there was the inner dialogue of the character and his prayers that his son would be okay: "Please, God, please, God, let him be okay." Along with these two streams of prayer, a third one was occurring as well.

Someone I had worked with came into my heart and mind. I suddenly realized this scene was meant to be an act of intercession for her as well. It was a mystery, but I knew that amidst the fiction being portrayed, something very real and healing could take place if the scene were lifted up to God as an offering. These prayers, along with the Jesus Prayer, allowed me to enter into the emotional, spiritual, and creative atmosphere that was necessary to perform these scenes.

I ended up talking to this person weeks later and revealed that she had been on my mind during those particular scenes and that I had been praying for her. She was quite surprised and blessed by the thought. Imagine if more artists were praying for others in this way. Imagine the synergy of prayer and compassion that would be created. The monks of Mount Athos (a semi-autonomous monastic republic in northeastern Greece), as well as other monks and nuns around the world, ceaselessly pray for the life of the world—they pray for all to participate in God.

This brings us back to the spiritual motif of prayer as intercession and the story of Job. Here is what the Almighty says to rebuke Job's friends:

> "And My servant Job shall pray for you. For I will accept him, lest I deal with you *according to your* folly; because you have not spoken of Me *what* is right, as My servant Job *has*." So Eliphaz the Temanite and Bildad the Shuhite *and* Zophar the Naamathite went and did as the Lord commanded them; for the Lord had accepted Job. (Job 42:7–9)

This is what intercessory prayer means. Job's prayers released mercy upon his friends. He was imitating Christ. So must the artist. The Epistle of St. James confirms this when it says,

"The effective, fervent prayer of a righteous man avails much" (James 5:16). St. Peter also echoes this truth: "For the eyes of the Lord are on the righteous, and His ears *are open* to their prayers" (1 Peter 3:12).

Again and again in the Scriptures, we read about the intercession of a few on behalf of the many. Moses stood before God and pleaded to be killed so the people of Israel might be spared. An angel visited Daniel toward the end of the Babylonian Captivity, telling him to pray, because the time of deliverance was at hand.

"The time is at hand; therefore pray!" This is the spiritual vision of the Scriptures, and it must become the vision of the artist. God has chosen to operate in cooperation with humanity and with our prayers. He has chosen to interact with His creation. He has chosen to be in relationship with humanity. The gift of fellowship with the Holy Trinity has given man an unparalleled blessing and responsibility. Moses prayed and the Lord had mercy. Daniel prayed and Israel was freed. Job prayed and his friends were spared. But all of these instances were only foreshadowings of the ultimate act of prayer and intercession.

THE ART OF THE CROSS

The ultimate act of intercession for the world is the Cross of Christ. Everything before this event points toward it, and everything since refers back to it. It is the center of history.

The artist is called to become a coworker with Christ in this profound grace (see 1 Cor. 3:9).

The artist's performances are destined to become not only seamless acts of prayer but also holy acts of intercession. The spiritual artist creates from a place of wounded love and humility—like Christ. She enters into the emotional, spiritual, and psychological plight of humanity, all the while praying that this living sacrifice would be acceptable and pleasing to God—that it would loose the bonds of the oppressed and give sight to the blind.

If the actor's role is that of someone struggling with suicide, then she becomes a living prayer for those who are oppressed by this particular darkness. If it happens to be that of a heroin addict, the artist's soul begins to cry out for those who are bound by this affliction. It does not need to be this dramatic all the time—but there will always be a place for some kind of cosmic compassion and intercession, whether in poetry, fiction, painting, sculpting, singing, dance, or any other artistic medium.

Without this dimension, the artist's performances and works of art remain self-indulgent, as far as her own spirit is concerned. God will still use these works of art because He is "all and in all." But how much more occurs when the artist consciously partners with the Divine? When she enters into synergy with God?

The more the artist allows herself to be broken in the presence of God's love, the more available she becomes to the mystery of the Spirit. Christ said, "You are the light of the world"

(Matt. 5:14). The artist must therefore shine—not through ego or self-righteousness, but through compassion, sacrifice, and love. Truth means nothing unless it is consumed with love. The artist must become "all flame," as one of the Desert Fathers proclaimed.[20] The soul is consumed by the passion of God's love for His creation.

The artist weeps all the time, not just when the cameras are rolling or when she's on stage singing a song. She sacrifices herself, not for recognition, but for the spiritual freedom of others. She weeps with those who weep and rejoices with those who rejoice. She becomes truly meek, which means to become sensitive and vulnerable to the Holy Spirit. The best example of this, after Christ Himself, is Mary the Theotokos (which literally means "God-Bearer").

ART AS SECRECY: THE WISDOM OF MARY

A Sword Will Pierce Your Very Soul

Traditional Christianity teaches that the Mother of God is an image of the Church and the Second Eve. She is the Mother of the New Creation, which is found in Christ, the Second Adam. Mary was the first to receive the Savior and walk intimately with Him: she was the first Christian. By contemplating her love of God and response to the Holy Spirit, the artist will undoubtedly increase in vulnerability to the Trinity.

Mary is contemplative and inwardly aware of spiritual realities. When something of great significance is revealed to her, she accepts the will of God and often says nothing: "But Mary kept all these things and pondered *them* in her heart" (Luke 2:19). She is an example for the artist in her willingness to suffer on behalf of others.

There is a very dramatic passage in the Gospel of Luke. The aging prophet Simeon had waited all his life to see the Messiah in the flesh. Upon seeing the Christ Child, he worshipped God and prophesied to Mary: "Then Simeon blessed them, and said to Mary His mother, 'Behold, this *Child* is destined for the fall and rising of many in Israel, and for a sign which will be spoken against (yes, a sword will pierce through your own soul also), that the thoughts of many hearts may be revealed'" (Luke 2:34–35).

Somehow, the suffering of this Child, the sword (the Cross) that was to pierce Mary's own soul, will reveal the secret thoughts of many hearts. Through suffering, revelation and liberation will occur. But not random or meaningless suffering—only suffering that is caught up and assimilated into the Cross of Christ.

As a child of the new creation, the artist is to become like Mary: a God-bearer, fully open to the mysterious and challenging will of God. If she, the Theotokos, is an image of the Church and a light of intercession for every person, then the artist must conclude that "a sword will pierce through her own soul also," so that the secret thoughts of others may be revealed. This, again, is the intercession of love and compassion we have been discussing. The artist also "takes up her own cross" and follows Christ.

Through love, she begins to share in the sufferings of Christ, as did His Mother. The artist finds herself at the foot of the Cross with Mary, weeping for the sorrow of her Son. This sorrow is the mourning of humanity itself; another melody in the symphony of the artist's vocation.

If she allows herself to become open to God and suffer for the brilliance of love, then the representative anguish of her performances and works of art will be joined with the prayers of the saints and will reveal the secret thoughts of those who witness them. If she allows herself to become a God-bearer (through repentance and the grace of the Holy Spirit), then every moment of every scene or every note of every song becomes a prophetic offering of worship and thanksgiving.

A great artist once said, "Always carry a secret with you." This is the wisdom of Mary—the wisdom of those who wish to create in the Spirit. One must carry a secret in order to reveal one.

From this place of ceaseless prayer and compassionate intercession, the artist is transformed from a mere entertainer into a prophet—a humble vessel of clay for God's love to dwell in. In the following chapter, we will meditate on the gift of silence and the role of contemplation in the life of the artist.

All Must Transcend

The artist must transcend, or he will die. But is not the artist simply a portrait of mankind, hung on the walls of reality, placed in the Colosseum of time for everyone to look at and remember—to remember that we all must transcend?

The soldier, the doctor, the priest and professor, the young, the old, the ugly and tamed . . . the winner, the loser, the prophet and famed . . . the cynic, the lover, the liberal and Jew, the broken, the lustful, the meditating Buddhist too . . . all who speak poems, sing songs, or fantasize—all who seek a look, a kiss, or an orgasm, all who read to be transported into the heat of another world, all who wish to stop time or go back to their youth, all who weep at the loss of an evolved ape, all who stick needles into their skin and fly away . . . all who debate, argue, and curse, all who study the Scriptures, the Pyramids, or the Universe, all who pray, wander, and seethe, all of Adam's children who move or breathe— every Utopian author from Moses to Marx . . . every news anchor, street-sweeper or pilot, every janitor, lawyer and judge, every student, thief, or martyr who wouldn't budge . . . everyone, everyone, whether in joy or sorrow, imagination or intellect, wisdom or naivety, holiness or nirvana, crucifixion or law, all must break through some shadow or wall, look beyond, above, or within . . . gaze past a visible horizon, an altar, or a trend, wound something, tear something, or mend . . . all must become something in the end, all who live must receive and send, all must place their fire somewhere and contend, all must kill their enemies or become their friend, all must separate or slowly blend, kiss the scars of laughter or on a reign of bitterness depend, all must worship, praise and defend . . . all must flicker in the borrowed night of existence, raging with obstinacy or with a burning humility bend—all must transcend.

4

ART AS

Listening

*If there were a little more silence, if we all kept
quiet . . . maybe we could understand something.*

FEDERICO FELLINI[21]

One of the first things an actor learns is the importance of listening. Working with Genie Francis as an eleven-year-old awakened me to the power of listening. All I had to do was watch and listen, and the entire performance would work itself out in the process. She was so emotionally available that nearly everything I did was a simple response to her. I began to realize the power and the fun of surprising the other person in the middle of a scene. Her motherly presence shaped me as an artist in ways I am only now beginning to understand. Her presence was like that of Mary, the Theotokos; she protected and nurtured me as a young artist.

Both Genie and Tony (Anthony Geary) would improvise quite a bit. It didn't take long for me to join in. I would save certain unscripted lines of dialogue until we were actually shooting the scene. Sometimes they were funny additions, and other times they were dramatic: slamming the table unexpectedly, throwing a bit of sarcasm in a place one wouldn't expect it, and so on. Tony was always changing his lines, trying to throw me off guard. It was great fun. But there was a deep truth to be discovered in this: It is impossible to be in the moment if you are not listening.

This training came in handy years later when I worked with Al Pacino in the film *Insomnia*. We worked on a particular scene over the course of two days, doing take after take after take. Not long into it, he began changing certain lines, adding strange and unexpected moments into the scene. I loved it. I had grown up in that kind of environment and found it to be invigorating. This sort of thing is especially important when you're doing a scene over and over again, and it becomes difficult to keep it fresh. Changing things up helps to keep the artist alert and present. But in order for it to work, both people have to be listening to each other. Otherwise, the scene will simply break down. Mr. Pacino would start throwing out obscure lines—I didn't even understand what some of them meant. He even started singing at one point. It was great!

The next day, we were filming his coverage, and I decided (young as I was) to give it right back to him. So periodically, I would add lines of dialogue that weren't scripted. I don't think he was expecting that from such a young actor, but he wasn't offended. In fact, I think he loved it. I didn't ask permission; we never spoke about this—I just did it. It forced us to continue to listen to each other—even into the fiftieth take of the scene.

The truth of listening is applicable for all forms of art and not simply acting. In order to write a song, you have to listen for the melody; you have to listen for the most truthful poetic structure of what is being created in the lyric. Bono has pointed out that a guitar player has to have faith that he will hear the next note he's supposed to play. He has to listen intently for the next move. He also has to listen to what the drummer is playing; just ask my brother. Every nuance the other musician brings changes how you perform. A writer has to listen to the voices of the characters he or she is creating. Why is it that writers like to go to secluded places to write? Why are artists often introverted? Why do they commonly feel as if they are alone, even when surrounded by many people? Artists were created to be listeners, and the noise of the world can easily drown out what they are listening for.

Sometimes it is necessary to go off to a secluded place in order to create. The best time to write songs (at least, in my own experience) is late at night or early in the morning, when everyone else is asleep. There is a silence and a calm throughout the entire house that lends itself to contemplation. I can hear myself think, and suddenly sparks of inspiration begin to rise to the surface. It's a wonderful time to pray and also to create without being anxious.

THE WOMB OF SILENCE

Listening is the beginning of creating. It is also the genesis of life. The artist comes into this world unable to speak intelligibly. But he has already begun to learn the sacred art of listening within the temple of his mother's womb. It is here that he first learns the eternal comfort of silence and listening. The infant listens to the rhythmic heartbeat and rushing blood of his mother. He can hear the vibrations and muted voices of those on the outside, whom he has yet to see with his eyes. He learns to move and feel, to receive nourishment, all before he is able to speak. It is within this silent temple that the artist is formed and made in the Image of the Divine. In the mystical words of the Psalmist:

> For You formed my inward parts;
> You covered me in my mother's womb.
> I will praise You, for I am fearfully *and* wonderfully made;
> Marvelous are Your works,
> And *that* my soul knows very well.
> My frame was not hidden from You,
> When I was made in secret,
> And skillfully wrought in the lowest parts of the earth.
> Your eyes saw my substance, being yet unformed.
> And in Your book they all were written,
> The days fashioned for me,
> When *as yet there were* none of them.
> How precious also are Your thoughts to me, O God!
> How great is the sum of them! (Psalm 139:13–17)

The artist was formed and fashioned to listen (from the internal place of his spirit) to the Spirit of God. He was given two ears and one mouth, as many parents have pointed out to their rambunctious children throughout the ages. This is a profound lesson from nature. If human beings listened twice as much as we spoke, what kind of world would we inhabit?

The ancient prophet Elijah discovered that the voice of the Almighty was not to be found in the ways one might expect:

> And behold, the Lord passed by, and a great and strong wind tore into the mountains and broke the rocks in pieces before the Lord, *but* the Lord *was* not in the wind; and after the wind an earthquake, *but* the Lord *was* not in the earthquake; and after the earthquake a fire, *but* the Lord *was* not in the fire; and after the fire a still small voice. (1 Kings 19:11–12)

Another translation reads, "a sound—a thin silence." A low whisper, a sound, a thin silence. This is how a person meets God? Is this what Jesus meant when He said, "Most assuredly, I say to you, unless one is born again, he cannot see the kingdom of God" (John 3:3)?

Was He speaking of a spiritual womb? Perhaps He meant that man must re-enter the womb of silence and rediscover life as a temple of grace and divine nourishment. Man must be born of "water and the Spirit." These words, again, are in keeping with the imagery of a womb. Man will have to learn a completely new language of existence.

In this place of comfort, solitude, and provision, the artist will begin to hear the low whisper of the Spirit and to grow in the intimacy of the Trinity. This is where he discovers the gift of silence.

THE GIFT OF SILENCE

Silence teaches the artist to listen—it creates space inside of him to discover secrets and encounter mysteries. To be silent before anything or anyone is an act of humility. Contrary to what our culture believes, humility (second only to love) is the strongest virtue of man. Silence breeds humility, and humility breeds true confidence, because it knows its own weakness. Humility has no reason to hide or falsify itself.

Therefore, silence teaches the artist how to tell the truth. It allows him to be in awe of something other than himself. It reveals his loneliness and his desires. It brings him back to the beginning of what makes him who he is: a person who is incredibly frail and yet mysteriously loved beyond measure.

The Desert Fathers taught that words spoken from silence possess their true nature. Words that come from the noise and anxiety of the world are only caricatures of authentic words. Take, for instance, that common childish game in which someone repeats the same word over and over until it loses all meaning and sounds completely senseless. Silence does the opposite. It reawakens the power of words, like the Tomb before the Resurrection or the night sky before a radiant dawn. Saint Ignatius of Antioch said, "A man who has truly mastered the utterances of Jesus will also be able to apprehend his silence, and thus reach full spiritual maturity, so that his words have the force of actions and his silences the significance of speech."[22]

Silence is a purifying medicine. The artist needs silence in order to see and hear properly—in order to recover his true nature. This invitation to silence is a gift of love that will continually lead him to a deeper purity of heart and vision. The artist is aware that only the pure in heart shall see God (see Matt. 5:8).

As the Psalmist David wrote, "Be still, and know that I am God" (Psalm 46:10). It is in the silence of prayer that the artist encounters the mystery of Love and his own true identity.

THE ART OF LISTENING

Many times Christ affirmed the significance (and the necessity) of listening. One example occurred when He was asked to rebuke someone for sitting at His feet in silence instead of serving dinner. This is a wonderful illustration of the weight God places on listening:

> Now it happened as they went that He entered a certain village; and a certain woman named Martha welcomed Him into her house. And she had a sister called Mary, who also sat at Jesus' feet and heard His word. But Martha was distracted with much serving, and she approached Him and said, "Lord, do You not care that my sister has left me to serve alone? Therefore tell her to help me."
>
> And Jesus answered and said to her, "Martha, Martha, you

are worried and troubled about many things. But one thing
is needed, and Mary has chosen that good part, which will
not be taken away from her." (Luke 10:38–42)

This is a picture of man's two natures: one is attuned to the
low whispers of God; the other defines its value and worth by
the sum of its activity and function. The latter is attuned to
the noise and anxiety of the world. The former is aware of the
eternal moment with God.

Christ is reorienting humanity. He is reminding the artist
that he is inherently a relational being, created for divine communion. Whatever functions the artist performs, they are to
remain in subordination to this beautiful truth of his nature.
Life begins with listening and being, not speaking and doing.
The artist's words and deeds become authentic and purified
only when they become manifest out of his inner communion
with God.

Again, Mary, the Mother of God, becomes a radiant example of this silence. By receiving Christ, the Life of the World,
into her womb in contemplative awe of God, she paved the
way for the whole world to reenter the spiritual womb of
heaven. The artist can now begin again, as it were, as a new
creation in Christ, through the grace of the Holy Spirit.

Mary's Song, known as the *Magnificat*, was sung from
her deep reverence and devotion to God. It came from her
silence. It is still being sung today by millions throughout the
world: "My soul magnifies the Lord, and my spirit rejoices
in God my Savior!" (Luke 1:46–47). These words carry the

weight of someone who is fully alive within—a soul who has received the gift of heaven and cannot bear to keep silent another moment. She sings for no one except her Savior and God; and yet she sings for the life of the world.

The Inner Dialogue of the Soul

The artist's words, songs, or paintings must be birthed out of silence if they are to carry the creative and spiritual weight he desires. In a practical sense, this teaches him that the outward expression of his art is always the result of his internal life. Christ, the Word of God, must first be awakened within him and speak within his heart before his mouth publishes the written dialogue or melody.

The icon known as *St. John in Silence* reveals the apophatic nature of the apostle's life and writings. He was immersed in the silence of God—he lived in the power of this mystery, embracing what could never be fully known or revealed. This is perhaps one of the reasons St. John was given the Revelation of Jesus Christ—because only one who lives in the silence of God can reveal Him to the world.

What is being spoken or displayed is always of less importance than the silence that precedes it. Human beings are running either toward silence or away from it. A question the artist might ask himself is this: Am I covering up my fear of silence by excessive noise and activity? Or am I running toward it in search of true freedom?

Every line of dialogue spoken or verse written should have a myriad of thoughts and prayers to assist and sustain it. The artist must become alive and authentic on the interior plane to become alive and authentic on the exterior plane. This is the only way to change the atmosphere of the world around us. This is true in both art and life. The hidden, unseen life sustains the visible and tangible life.

Inner dialogue precedes its outward expression. Silence is the food of the artist's interior life.

THE GIFT OF CONTEMPLATION

Contemplation awakens the realization that we are not alone. It is also the realm where the artist encounters the majesty of his true freedom as a human being. It is only in the presence of the One who fashioned him in His Divine Image that the artist glimpses the intrinsic depth of his own personhood—where he experiences the profound and soul-shaking revelation of choice and free will.

In contemplation, the artist traverses beyond the surface of existence into the realm of encountering God—not as an abstract idea, but as the Other who has always been. From this internal state of communion, he begins to learn and perceive the gift of responding to God—instead of merely reacting to the circumstances of life as a default. Contemplation does not consist merely of moments of serenity, but also of a fight to surrender. Contemplation is where the artist embraces the majesty of God, which leads to lasting peace and spiritual victory over chaos.

In *Encountering the Mystery*, Ecumenical Patriarch Bartholomew writes, "Silence is in fact constructive, not passive."[23] He then goes on to say that silence includes surrender and sacrifice:

> Surrender and sacrifice mean giving up our pride, passions, and selfish desires; at the same time, they imply embracing the virtues that constitute the other side of that coin, namely love and generosity. In fact, surrender and sacrifice are ways of achieving inner peace, through which everyone and everything around us find common serenity.[24]

Silence and contemplation are the entrance into the inner temple of the Most High. The Kingdom of heaven is within the artist through the grace of the Holy Spirit. This reality empowers the artist to soar to creative heights he never thought possible. It gives him the confidence to explore, to take risks, and to step out in faith, because he knows he is not alone.

This inner communion with God emboldens the soul into a state of authentic joy. The artist rejoices, "I am not alone. I was created for an epic voyage—a voyage of repentance and discovery—to discover the gifts and blessings of God in the depths of my own heart. My soul is not alone." This is the miracle of being made in the Image of God.

Out of silence, the Word of God spoke, "Let there be light!" and the world was made. It is the same for the artist, who is made in His Image: He mimics Christ, the Word of

God, by engaging in the mystery of prayer and silence. From this sacred place, he speaks as a royal priest over the whole world and into its very fabric, echoing the divine commission, "Let there be light!" Indeed, creation is an ongoing manifestation of the glory and goodness of God. Even amidst the fearsome darkness, the Light shines; and those who receive the Light become conscious partakers in the divine nature, becoming "the light of the world."

> "You are the light of the world. A city that is set on a hill cannot be hidden. Nor do they light a lamp and put it under a basket, but on a lampstand, and it gives light to all *who are* in the house. Let your light so shine before men, that they may see your good works and glorify your Father in heaven." (Matt. 5:14–16)

This, however, will require something of the artist—something greater than his self-reliance and ego: it will require his humility and his belief in something greater than himself. The subject of the following chapter will be how the gift of faith relates to the life of the artist.

5

ART AS BELIEF:

What Is the Vital Organ?

There is nothing impossible unto those who believe;
lively and unshaken faith can accomplish great
miracles in the twinkling of an eye.

ST. JOHN OF KRONSTADT[25]

When the artist begins to write a song, he must possess an incredible amount of faith, which precedes the final result. Perhaps a particular lyric suddenly appeared in his head when he woke up that morning. Or a vague melody mysteriously drifted into his conscious thought. Still, a song does not exist—only the very beginnings or the possibility of a song. In order to create an actual song, the artist must believe that one exists—he just hasn't discovered it yet.

When the artist sits down and plays the first few chords of an unwritten song, she must believe that somehow the path will open up as she goes. There are those magical moments when an entire song emerges in one sitting, but these are few and far between. "You Didn't Win" was a song like that for me. I sat down at the piano, played the chords for the first time, sang the words for the first time, and the entire thing was done in a matter of minutes. This song was born out of great suffering, and perhaps that is why it was birthed so simply. But most of time, it takes hours and days, even months before it all comes together. Why would anyone keep working on something that seems to be a dead end everywhere she turns? Because deep down the artist believes there is a song to be found. She can't see it, but she knows it's there. Creation takes belief.

The inspiration for the song "The Coming Dawn" came from watching Bob Dylan and Roy Orbison write music in *The Traveling Wilburys.* Bob Dylan sat down, strummed a couple of chords, and said, "Let's try one like this?" I laughed and thought, *Yeah, Bob, it's that easy, isn't it?* He didn't know where it was going. He simply believed something would occur. I had my guitar with me at the time, and I strummed a G chord and mocked him a little. Four hours later, I had written one of my favorite songs. It was a simple and childlike act of faith combined with inspiration from incredible artists and the synergy of the Holy Spirit.

Creating is the art of believing. The artist believes in the truth of what is occurring before she sees the result. It is an act of faith. There is a profound connection between faith and our spiritual efficacy: "Having then gifts differing according to the grace that is given to us, *let us use them*: if prophecy, *let us prophesy* in proportion to our faith" (Rom. 12:6).

The Christian prophesies according to his or her faith. This means that the artist creates according to her faith as well, because all true art is a form of prophecy. Faith is the vital organ or instrument within the artist. She must believe not only the fictional reality she is portraying, but also the spiritual reality of what is occurring; the actual event taking place all around her.

When the artist builds her entire life on faith, it becomes an incredible weapon for humanity in the fight for self-actualization in God. As she learns to abide with her Creator, to listen to the Holy Spirit, to fix her gaze on things unseen, she begins to realize that her preparation and formation is occurring every day, in and out of season.

When the faith of the artist is infused into the moment of creation, anything becomes possible. The event that is taking place becomes cosmic and relevant beyond the performance or piece of art itself. She does not put life on pause, so to speak, and perform. She brings her life into the performance and releases what she possesses within her heart. It is an act of faith and reliance on the Holy Spirit.

The artist needs faith, but she also needs wisdom. There are many paths that appear to offer her freedom along the way, but the prophetic artist is in a constant state of searching and discovering the Way of the Spirit. Studying the Scriptures and the lives of the saints is a vital way for her to remain pure in heart.

FROM MONOLOGUE TO TRIALOGUE: THE WAY OF THE TRINITY

Many things occur simultaneously in the life of the artist. I will use acting to illustrate this particular point. The inner life of the character and the inner life of the actor temporarily coexist. This skill is a paradoxical one. The spiritual actor hopes to unite these two realities, while at the same time keeping them separate.

What does this mean? It means the actor unites what is healthy and separates what is destructive. When these two distinctive realities become confused, personal crisis creeps in. Hence, the endless on-set romances, which usually die shortly after the film or play ends. Or the tragedy of a young actor who thinks experimenting with heroin is the only way to play a convincing addict. The young performer ends up dead only a few short years after his brilliant performance.

These lines must not be confused if the actor desires to remain an actor and not slowly morph into someone with multiple personality disorder. Without this clear distinction, the actor may (in subtle ways) actually become the character, because he has no real sense of his own identity. This is not the vocation of the spiritual artist. And it is a danger of method acting. The artist is called to bring the character to life while at the same time guarding the integrity of her own soul. This is part of the mystery of true acting.

These lines must remain distinct wherever they might cause harm. And yet the actor must also infuse the holy parts of his own personal nature into the creative process. Only then will freedom inhabit the performer. When the fictional intent of the character is brought into the spiritual intent of the artist, it becomes purified and sharpened. It becomes liberated. How is this possible? Only by the grace of the Holy Spirit and the repentance of the artist.

Let me share an example. When I was about seventeen years old, I played a heroin addict in a film. The experience was intense. One of the first things I had to do was learn about the drug itself: what it does to the body and the mind; what the short and long-term effects are. I had to climb into, so to speak, the body, psychology, and emotional turmoil of a young man who was losing everything because of his addiction. I have known people very close to me who have struggled for years with addiction, and it has left a permanent mark on my soul. For me, this role was not simply a performance, but a prayer for those who had suffered through something similar.

My character was crying out for the drug—but I was crying out for all those who had battled with addiction, as well as their family members. The fictional desire of the character was united (but not confused) with the actual desire of my heart as an artist, and the result (by God's grace) was a prophetic one.

I received many emails and letters for years afterward from people whose lives had been changed after watching that film. I never dabbled in the drug. By God's grace, my soul was not given over to darkness in order to portray this sickness. It was a spiritual performance of intercession.

The artist portrays confusion from an inner place of peace and trust. He portrays chaos and hatred from an inner place of love and mercy. These two realities appear contradictory on the surface; but they are not. Only the God of Love understands the full depth of human anguish and ecstasy. Christ was able to identify with us in our confusion and longing; He was able to enter into our suffering with the utmost empathy and compassion, precisely because His heart was filled with incomprehensible Light. Only Light can truly comprehend darkness. The more the artist beholds the nature of God, the more he comes to know himself. It is the face of Christ that reveals his true nature and opens his heart to compassion.

This is where the "third mode" or the Way of the Trinity breaks into our consciousness. There are three dimensions within the inner life of the artist. The best way to express them is through the medium of acting.

The progression is like this: The actor moves from an inner state of isolated monologue (egoism) to a more profound state of dialogue with others (humanism), and then ultimately into what Stephen Muse calls a "trialogue": the state of personal and cosmic communication with God, ourselves, and other persons. This threefold way is the place of original human radiance. "All the fruits of the garden of the cosmos are available to humanity. Only the tree that leads to knowledge obtained through monologue instead of trialogue with God and Creation is forbidden in order to protect creation from the suffering brought into being through the damage inherent to this path."[26]

In other words, the way of the artist is dynamic relational communion with God and creation. If the artist's life, prayers, and craft fail to lead her to the very depths of love, repentance, and resurrection, then she is not experiencing the fullness of her humanity. It is an empty display of vainglory.

From this relational state of belief, the artist approaches the nuances of her craft. Everything begins and ends with a cosmic perception of reality. She is not simply creating something to be admired; she is changing the atmosphere through communion with God. Without the gift of faith and the inspiration of love, these aspirations will remain abstract and impossible for the artist to fully attain.

ART AS PHILANTHROPY

The most brilliant artists possess the gift of faith, whether they are conscious or subconscious participants in this grace. "Christ is all and in all" (Col. 3:11), and those who believe must always affirm the Christ within their fellow artists and mentors. These people may not be consciously aware of the source of their gifts, but the artist will joyfully celebrate who God is within them, never judging or degrading the way they approach their craft or where they happen to be on their unique journey in life.

Fr. Thomas Hopko articulated this complex truth:

> A person's willingness to be God's artwork may not necessarily be conscious—or it may not necessarily even be consciously "Christian." It may derive from the person's love for and obedience to God's Law, written on their hearts. . . . It is also true that a person who is claiming to be "Christian" may in fact, not be Christian at all.[27]

Amen! The artist has much to learn from everyone she encounters. Humility is the way of Christ. To create "in the Spirit" also means to exude this kind of faith and love toward one's coworkers. What the artist discovers in contemplating the nature of God is His uncompromising philanthropy. This word has a much deeper meaning than its popular understanding. It originally was a definition of God. It means that the core of God's heart is *One who gives freely*. His heart is filled with an unselfish abundance of love and belief in His creation. It could be said that no man ever believes in God until it is first revealed in his soul that God believes in him.

This is the foundation of the artist's faith: the radical and unconditional love of God. This is her ethos and compass. Creating is an act of belief, not only in the Holy Spirit, but also in the goodness of those she is blessed to work with. This extends beyond her fellow actors, directors, musicians, or writers to everyone she encounters. Everyone is included in God's philanthropy. This will keep the artist open to the creative workings of the Holy Spirit. This allows her truly to become a holistic performer who continually experiences the creativity of love.

The Scriptures declare, "But without faith *it is* impossible to please [God]" (Heb. 11:6). Faith sees into the heart of things. By its very nature, faith is able to go beneath the surface of an event and find something holy to praise and exalt. It is able to look beyond the outward demeanor and glimpse the sacredness of creation. Faith brings the artist back to the childlike state of acceptance and boldness. Only by faith can we encounter the mystery of God's love in other people.

Repeatedly, Christ said, "Your faith has saved you" (Luke 7:50) or "your faith has made you well" (Luke 18:42). Whenever the artist is challenged by her own limitations and insecurities, she can remember these words. They reveal a secret every artist is invited to experience. It is faith that pulls her out of the momentary abyss of confusion or turmoil. It is faith that restores her confidence and freedom. Faith emboldens the artist to receive the revelation that nothing is accidental or meaningless. Every moment filled with faith becomes a universal moment: a moment of eternal significance.

One sees this reality in Christ's response to a crucial question: "What shall we do, that we may work the works of God?" Jesus answered them, "This is the work of God, that you believe" (John 6:28–29). If one were to ask this question in regard to an artist's vocation, the response would doubtless be the same.

Through Jesus' answer to this question: "What shall we do,

that we may work the works of God?" He reveals to the artist that God's vision of belief is not merely a sentiment but an all-encompassing action of the heart, mind, body, and soul. It is a holistic action of surrender and love. For Christ, faith is more than an intellectual agreement. It ultimately means more than verbal consent. Faith is alive and active: "What shall we do?" His response: *Believe*. "For as the body without the spirit is dead, so faith without works is dead also" (James 2:26).

The question could be paraphrased for the sake of our thesis: "What must the artist do to create prophetic works of art?" Christ's answer would again be: *Believe*. The Son of God is the beginning and the end of the artist's creative vision: not religion per se, or the traditions of men, but Christ Himself as revealed through the Holy Tradition of the Apostles. This is true because Christ is the very Image and Revelation of God. He is the "author and finisher of *our* faith" (Heb. 12:2). The artist believes, not only *in* Christ, but also *through* Him. And this is made possible by the work of the Holy Spirit. The artist's desire and inspiration are caught up in a Trinitarian dance. She *man*ufactures nothing. The spiritual artist receives blessing upon blessing and grace upon grace from her intimacy with the Holy Trinity. As Michelangelo said, "The true work of art is but a shadow of the divine perfection."[28] This sacred dance of faith is the only thing truly pleasing to the Divine. It is the only creative process that leads to lasting peace and fulfillment.

The artist is a responder and discoverer—not an autonomous god, quickly given over to various delusions of boasting or endless psychological episodes of insecurity. Faith is a gift the artist receives in complete innocence, and through this grace even she, a mere child at heart, may work the works of God.

6

ART AS

Prophecy

All true beauty has the power to draw the soul towards Thee, and to make it sing in ecstasy: Alleluia!

AKATHIST HYMN, GLORY TO GOD FOR ALL THINGS[29]

In the mid-nineties I was placed into a storyline that would forever change my life for the better. I was about fifteen years old, and the subject matter was extreme, especially for teenagers. The story centered on a young girl who had been raped. My character found her crawling out of the bushes in the snow; her dress was torn, and her eyes were frightened and full of tears.

As a young artist, I had to contemplate such devastation on the soul of an innocent girl. It broke my heart, just the thought of it. I discovered that my preparation for these scenes (the storyline went on for a couple of years) involved asking God some very tough questions. "How could You let this happen? Why didn't You do anything to stop it? How can I trust You, if You allow things like this to happen to innocent people? How do I know You're good? I can't handle the depth of pain I feel when I look into her eyes. What can I do to help her get through this?"

This storyline of romance, healing, purity, and redemption captivated a large audience and changed the lives of many who tuned in. I received letters for many years afterward from people who had suffered through similar circumstances. Their hearts were touched in profound ways by the love and hero-ism of the character I was portraying. In my heart, I knew what they were drawn to was Christ Himself and not the actor portraying the hero. My prayer was that Christ would radi-ate and draw people to Himself through His grace and my unworthy cooperation.

Years later, at a fan event, I had the opportunity to share with the people present why I believed that storyline meant so much to them. I said their hearts were drawn to the beauty of healing, compassion, purity, redemption, and love—they were drawn to Christ. That storyline was prophetic in that it dis-played a sacred and divine romance that reflected Christ and the Church. This made me realize that every story is a parable of light and darkness, and every work of art has the potential to become prophetic. I say *potential*, because it is not a given.

Without the Eternal Poet's presence, art is transcendent

only to the point of overcoming the mundane; it cannot impart the transfiguration of the Divine. It is possible for art to possess a false light, in which its beauty lures one beyond himself toward an idol. When art itself is worshipped, instead of valued as a sacramental gift whereby man can glorify God, it becomes a mirage. Art can awaken, it can inspire, it can even begin to heal—but it cannot complete any of these movements. It is not the Absolute.

Paul Evdokimov put it this way:

> Sooner or later, thought, art and social life reach their own limits, and then a choice is imposed: to be located in the infinity of their own immanence, to be intoxicated by their own emptiness, or to surpass their strangulating limitations and, in the transparency of clear waters to reflect the transcendent. God desires this. His kingdom is not accessible, except through the chaos of this world.[30]

Creating is meant to be a form of prophecy. But what kind of prophecy? For our purposes, I mean the gift of receiving and sharing the heart of God for humanity. Prophecy is the mystery of God communicating His nature and will through us. (The more common understanding of prophecy includes the gift of seeing into the future; but this is a particular charismatic gift that is currently not our focus.)

To be prophetic means to live in communion with the Spirit. His intentions become the artist's intentions, through ceaseless prayer, love-filled repentance, and the transformation of the mind. To be prophetic means to be present with God.

This is the truest measure of being in the moment. The artist becomes so alive to the whispers of the Spirit that he loses sight of himself and enters into authentic creativity and spiritual authority.

THE ETHOS OF THE ARTIST

There is a very strong connection between the artist and the Holy Spirit. In the Scriptures, the first time it was ever recorded that someone was "filled with the Holy Spirit" was in Exodus. This person was an artist, called to work on God's Temple:

> Then the Lord spoke to Moses, saying: "See, I have called
> by name Bezalel the son of Uri, the son of Hur, of the tribe
> of Judah. And I have filled him with the Spirit of God, in
> wisdom, in understanding, in knowledge, and in all *manner of*
> workmanship, to design artistic works, to work in gold, in sil-
> ver, in bronze, in cutting jewels for setting, in carving wood,
> and to work in all *manner of* workmanship." (Ex. 31:1–5)

This is the ethos of the artist. It is the Spirit who fills him with the ability, intelligence, knowledge, and craftsmanship to do the things he is destined to do. But many things are required of him to grow in heavenly creativity.

One of the essential virtues of the prophetic artist is wisdom. But like Truth, the Wisdom of God is not an abstract thing, but a Person: Jesus Christ. The Wisdom of Christ is not at all like the wisdom of this world. The Wisdom of the Son is

shown, not in worldly pomp or vanity, but in utter humility—
the humility of the Cross.

> For the message of the cross is foolishness to those who are
> perishing, but to us who are being saved it is the power of
> God. For it is written:
>> "I will destroy the wisdom of the wise,
>> And bring to nothing the understanding of the prudent."
> Where is the wise? Where is the scribe? Where is the
> disputer of this age? Has not God made foolish the wisdom
> of this world? For since, in the wisdom of God, the world
> through wisdom did not know God, it pleased God through
> the foolishness of the message preached to save those who
> believe. For Jews request a sign, and Greeks seek after wis-
> dom; but we preach Christ crucified, to the Jews a stumbling
> block and to the Greeks foolishness, but to those who are
> called, both Jews and Greeks, Christ the power of God and
> the wisdom of God. Because the foolishness of God is wiser
> than men, and the weakness of God is stronger than men.
> (1 Cor. 1:18–25)

To be a prophetic artist, one must continually lose sight of
oneself and become awakened to the majesty of God. Humility is simply a description of this awakening.

"The fear of the Lord is the beginning of wisdom, / And the
knowledge of the Holy One is understanding" (Prov. 9:10). The
term "the fear of the Lord" does not refer to a coercive fear
like that of an unloved slave. It means the reverence and awe
that belong to a much-loved child standing before his stronger
and wiser father. This "fear of the Lord" is the beginning of

wisdom because it is honest and pure. It is simply right and proper and lends itself to intimacy. The Holy One is above man and infinitely more knowledgeable and wise. The wisdom of humility must guide the artist's creative and prophetic journey.

CREATING IN THE WISDOM OF THE SON

Christ's relationship with the Father is the artist's model for spiritual and creative dynamism: "Then Jesus answered and said to them, 'Most assuredly, I say to you, the Son can do nothing of Himself, but what He sees the Father do; for whatever He does, the Son also does in like manner. For the Father loves the Son, and shows Him all things that He Himself does; and He will show Him greater works than these, that you may marvel'" (John 5:19–20).

The artist is living not for or from himself, but through the power of the Trinity. When the artist abandons the illusion of autonomy, he becomes a vessel of the Divine Flame. He enters into Christ's relationship with His Father. He learns the humility of the Son. Only then will he radiate like Him: in the power and self-emptying of the Holy Trinity.

The prophet Isaiah speaks of this correlation:

And *though* the Lord gives you
The bread of adversity and the water of affliction,
Yet your teachers will not be moved into a corner anymore,
But your eyes shall see your teachers.
Your ears shall hear a word behind you, saying,

"This is the way, walk in it,"
Whenever you turn to the right hand
Or whenever you turn to the left. (Is. 30:20–21)

To create prophetically means to receive the anointing of the Spirit and actively grow in humility and sensitivity to the mercies of God. It is through the "bread of adversity and the water of affliction" that the artist learns to see his Teacher and hear His Voice, quietly saying, "This is the way, walk in it."

It is not through human striving, nor through worldly success that the artist begins to live prophetically. It comes with heartbreak—when all the false pretensions of glory and prowess fall to the ground and shatter. It happens when love penetrates the heart and reigns in the soul.

The foundation of this powerful dynamic is love—not function. "For the Father loves the Son and shows him all that he himself is doing." The Father loves the Son. This is Christ's ethos, and (by grace) it can become the artist's as well. Everything man does is empowered by the reality that he is loved beyond measure. He is loved and accepted as Christ was loved and accepted by His Father. Man has been given Christ's life, while his old life was crucified with Christ on the Cross. Love is received only by the humble. And the gift of mercy is embraced only by the vulnerable and meek. Hence the words of St. Paul in regards to our Savior:

> Let this mind be in you which was also in Christ Jesus, who, being in the form of God, did not consider it robbery to be equal with God, but made Himself of no reputation, taking

the form of a bondservant, *and* coming in the likeness of
men. And being found in appearance as a man, He humbled
Himself and became obedient to *the point of* death, even the
death of the cross. Therefore God also has highly exalted
Him and given Him the name which is above every name.
(Phil. 2:5–9)

As Patriarch Jeremiah II of Constantinople said, "Humility is
aroused by the descent of God, the Logos, from the heavens."[31] Humility is the only way to prophetically create in the
Spirit. Jesus said, "Come to Me, all *you* who labor and are
heavy laden, and I will give you rest. Take My yoke upon you
and learn from Me, for I am gentle and lowly in heart, and
you will find rest for your souls" (Matt. 11:28–29). Humility
means to live in the purity of man's original design. Christ is
the Image of what it means to truly be human and He is inde-
scribably humble and selfless.

He also said this mysterious phrase: "I do not receive honor
from men. . . . How can you believe, who receive honor from
one another, and do not seek the honor that *comes* from the
only God?" (John 5:41, 44).

"How can you believe, who receive honor from one
another?" What a remarkable question. What does this mean
for the artist? It means there is a profound link between his
ability to believe and the state of humility within him. To
receive glory from the world immediately puts the heart at war
with the humility of Christ. It is an obstruction of pride. And
this obstruction wounds the artist's faith.

If Christ did not receive glory from people, why on earth should the artist? The strength of the artist's prophetic gift comes from the mystery of grace acting upon his weakness. He is always the recipient of God's philanthropy. St. Paul wrote: "And He said to me, 'My grace is sufficient for you, for My strength is made perfect in weakness.' Therefore most gladly I will rather boast in my infirmities, that the power of Christ may rest upon me" (2 Cor. 12:9).

The Scriptures also speak of the great humility of Moses: "Now the man Moses was very humble, more than all men who *were* on the face of the earth" (Num. 12:3). The same model is found in John the Baptist when he spoke of Christ: "There comes One after me who is mightier than I, whose sandal strap I am not worthy to stoop down and loose" (Mark 1:7).

From Moses to John the Baptist to Christ Himself, man is surrounded by the humility of the prophetic. There is no room for self-glorification—it is the way of the Cross, which leads to the Resurrection. When the soul glimpses the majesty of God, it becomes undone—suddenly aware of its own weakness and dependency. From this place, the brilliant force of God's love enters the heart, and the artist may begin.

ART AS REVELATION AND REPENTANCE

Some of the most amazing stories are ones of repentance and resurrection. The beauty of parables (which constituted one of Christ's essential modes of teaching) is that they fully engage the imagination of the listener. They compel him to actively participate in what is being revealed. When human beings witness a story, it is from a visceral place of inner dialogue and revelation.

The most powerful moments in film are those of repentance—when a character finally realizes what he or she most wants or desires; when he glimpses what is real and true. Like the prodigal son, he begins to run back home. This happens through various awakenings that lead to a character's resurrection. On the tragic side of story, it is the character's failure to embrace repentance that causes us to mourn as we witness a tragedy.

Archimandrite Aimilianos of Simonopetra, in *The Way of the Spirit*, explains that the spiritual life begins when the soul feels exiled from its real home. This sense of being exiled is the impetus for man's voyage home. This is the moment (or moments) when the soul encounters actual repentance. Not in the abstract, but in the form of a revolution. He goes on to say that the soul lives in a spiritual war between honesty and concealment. This is pertinent in the realm of character development and the authenticity of an artist.

Why do we so often choose to conceal and cover things up? For the simple reason that it is a terrible thing for us to realize that we are nothing. Do you know what it means to go from thinking that you're special and important, from being respected publicly, from thinking that you've done great things, from being talented, wonderful, good-looking, charming, and I don't know what else besides, to recognizing that,

on the contrary, you're naked and of no consequence what-
soever? It requires strength to accept that, a lot of strength.
And yet we can't even accept the slightest blemish that we
might have, or any fault, failure, error or sin that we may
have committed, without covering it up with a lie, and then
covering up that lie with a second one, and then the second
with a third.

A person may conceal his or her nakedness by means of an
inferiority complex, by acts of aggression, by self-justification,
by *donning various masks*, and by many other means. (emphasis mine)[32]

Human beings spend most of their lives "donning various
masks" to hide their weaknesses, fears, insecurities, and shame.
Repentance is simply the act of taking off the masks. This is
perhaps the hardest thing in the world for a person to do. But
one must remember that repentance is not an end in itself. It
always occurs in the framework of a glorious vision—a vision of
returning home—where one discovers or rediscovers his true
nature and identity. Repentance is not thinking horribly of
yourself and living in shame. Authentic repentance leads to the
liberation of the soul. Repentance is the door that enables the
artist to encounter the ecstasy of God's presence within him.

ART AS HONESTY AND CONCEALMENT

The characters the artist portrays in novels, acting, or song are
almost always shape-shifting, inhabiting one mask after another.
Their true self only temporarily rises to the surface in subtle

ways. It happens at various times for many reasons. Exploring human nature as an exiled being yearning for reconciliation is profound for the artist, especially in the realm of character development and empathy.

One of my first real explorations of these truths as an actor was during the film *The Deep End of the Ocean*. My character, Vincent, was tormented by the guilt of his little brother's disappearance. Vincent blamed himself because he was supposed to be watching his little brother when the boy was taken. This guilt haunted him for years afterward and was never vocalized to anyone—perhaps not even to himself. He had to conceal his guilt through various masks of sarcasm and apathy.

This film was based on a novel, and I benefited tremendously from reading it while we were filming. It got to the point that I would actually add a small line of dialogue into the script and then discover, a couple of weeks later, that this exact line was also in the novel! It was an immense help to explore the character in the form of a novel. So many moments and descriptions of concealment were expressed. It was beautifully written.

Around that same time, I became fascinated with the writings of Dostoevsky. Every artist should read Dostoevsky. He is a genius at revealing human nature—a master psychologist. At the same time, he was a person who suffered greatly in his life and found a deep and penetrating faith in Christ. Dostoevsky was a madman of sorts—but he was an artist who desired with everything in him to radiate the honesty of Jesus Christ amidst the suffering and insanity of the world. His books were prophetic. They foresaw what was to become of Russia if her people continued to forsake God and embrace the delusions of the Western intelligentsia. Through tragedy, he warned an entire nation; and his words still ring true for us today, if only we will listen.

In his writings, I discovered the power of repentance, contradiction, and paradox. I discovered how important these truths are to the artist. It is essential for the artist to be a man who embraces certain paradoxes.

"And it shall come to pass afterward
That I will pour out My Spirit on all flesh;
Your sons and your daughters shall prophesy,
Your old men shall dream dreams,
Your young men shall see visions.
And also on My menservants and on My maidservants
I will pour out My Spirit in those days." (Joel 2:28–29)

Every artist has been given a prophetic destiny. The artist has been given a substantial gift and responsibility: he is called to enter into the repentance of humanity, which ultimately leads to some form of resurrection and new life. In many ways, artists are the caretakers of the culture. As mentioned earlier, Plato is thought to have said, "Give me the songs of a nation, and it matters not who writes its laws."

Whether in music, painting, writing, acting, or any other art, artists have a unique responsibility to become prophetic mirrors of the zeitgeist, all the while pointing to an eternal kingdom. The artist has been given the charge to assist in awakening the true hunger inside each soul.

The more he allows himself to enter into a life of repentance, the more grace his heart will be able to receive. From this place of repentance, he becomes, as Christ declared, one of the "sons of the resurrection" (Luke 20:36).

The first words of Christ's public ministry were, "Repent, for the kingdom of heaven is at hand" (Matt. 3:2). The artist begins by daily receiving the gift of repentance. The most common translation of the Greek term for repentance, *metanoia*, is "change of heart or mind." But this fails to express the deeper meaning and intent of the word. In the opinion of Fr. John McGuckin, the term *metanoia* would best be translated "the act of becoming authentic."[33] The Scriptures say the prodigal son "came to his senses"—he returned to his right mind.

In this context, repentance means to see God differently and oneself as a new creation in Him. It means to rediscover the world as something that is infinitely loved and mysteriously known. As Norris J. Chumley writes, "We become authentic by surrendering our ego to God—admitting our flaws, failings, and sins—and thereby wiping the slate clean, as it were, before beginning a life of prayer and contemplation that will lead us to communion with God."[34]

The artist becomes a prophet of the Kingdom of heaven: a beacon of light, awakening a thirst for communion with the Holy Trinity. "For the earnest expectation of the creation eagerly waits for the revealing of the sons of God" (Rom. 8:19).

It is important to note that the artist is not in the business of moralizing or proselytizing. Some of his works of art may have overtly religious or spiritual themes; others may not. Contrived art for the sake of preaching to people is an offense to the mystery and sacredness of creation. Beauty and honesty are the primary inspirations of the artist: he trusts the grace and presence of the Holy Spirit to lead hearts into the truth. The prophetic artist is one who breaks open the remembrance of humanity, creating an atmosphere for the Spirit of God to breathe new life into creation.

In his profound book, *An Experiment in Criticism*, C. S. Lewis speaks of the power of great literature to expand the human experience. His words should not be limited to literature alone, but can easily be applied to all forms of art.

> Literary experience heals the wound, without undermining the privilege, of individuality. . . . In reading great literature I become a thousand men and yet remain myself. Like the night sky in the Greek poem, I see with a myriad eyes, but it is still I who see. Here, as in worship, in love, in moral action, and in knowing, I transcend myself; and am never more myself than when I do.[35]

The Lost Artist

Idle words and vain rhyme
Sail the leafy wind,
How sad it is, and subtle a crime,
When real life is starved to begin.
To scribble love's kaleidoscope
With poignant and courageous wit,
But never live the virtue praised
By many a crafted script.

Yes, I pity the poet
Who bleeds much ink, but little blood,
Whose mind worships beauty,
Whilst heart is covered in mud,
The painter who anoints his canvas,
Impassioned by Eros sublime,
But when brush is still
Has nothing to give
But a quiet, desperate sigh.
Indeed, I pity the actor who captivates
Through marvelous words given to say,
Then is sharp with child or spouse,
Who run from insult or fray,
The singer who consoles thousands,
With voice angelic and pure,
Yet, beneath the sound, no peace can be found,

Only a fleeting cure,
The comedian who dazzles the room,
But is miserable and dark within,
The dancer who glides on majestic waves,
Whilst courage of soul is thin.

Love!
Yes, love, be sought and released!
Your eyes are the sonnets your lover needs!
Love!
Yes, love, be praised and lived!
Your heart and soul are the higher gifts to give!
For these anointed talents, precious though
They be, are merely shadows, and echoes;
To arouse a hunger for the real and mighty thing!

———◆———

7

ART AS

Sacrament

O Heavenly King, Comforter, Spirit of Truth,
who are everywhere present and fill all things;
Treasury of Blessings, and Giver of Life:
Come and abide in us, and cleanse us from every
impurity, and save our souls, O Good One.

For the spiritual artist, one of the most beautiful realities is that the whole world is a sacrament. This reality penetrates every aspect of the artist's life. Contrary to what many religious voices have espoused, God the Artist is not against the body or the material world. Rather, He loves the world, which He created. From the moment He formed the world and laid eyes upon it, so to speak, He knew that it was "good" (Gen. 1:4). The meaning of this word in the Hebrew is "beautifully good!"

According to traditional Christianity, God is not anti-matter. He is pro-assimilation between the visible realm and the spiritual realm of heaven. Christ taught his Apostles to pray, "Your kingdom come. / Your will be done / On earth *as it* is in heaven" (Matt. 6:10).

The poetry of sacramental theology has been almost entirely ignored in our society, and the repercussions are manifest everywhere—especially in the arts. There is a sharp divorce between the natural and the spiritual. Our flesh and bones are seen as disposable material to be used for a short time and then discarded, instead of as mystical temples of the Divine. We see this in the way sex has been degraded into a purely physical action. It is no longer seen as pointing toward the Kingdom of heaven and the joy of Christ and His Church. It is simply two bodies, chemically attracted to one another, fulfilling a need. Love has almost nothing to do with it anymore. The two becoming one flesh is no longer a sacred mystery between a man and a woman for the rest of their lives—it is now commonplace, with interchangeable partners. Our society seems shocked when a lifestyle of numerous sexual relationships leads to emotional imbalance and increasing anxiety. Our bodies have successfully been detached from our souls.

We live in an either/or mentality and suffer from an ingrained dualism. We are missing out on the poetic depth of our nature. Traditional Christianity teaches that the whole world is a sacrament. This profound reality is transformative for artists. Artists are by nature sacramental. They instinctively believe in the mystery and spiritual nature of their craft.

The vision of mankind revealed by Orthodox Christianity is that man and woman are not spirits trapped in bodies, as the Platonists believe. Rather, humanity is a sacramental being that yearns for the redemption of the body. Without the body, man is not fully human. It is the union of realms that humanity desires.

The spiritual artist seeks to recover the mystery of God's blessing over the physical world and to create in the Spirit with authority. The body becomes one with the heart and the mind. Human beings are, in a very real sense, symphonic creatures.

How does this affect the life of the artist? It affects everything: The guitar he strums is not merely a piece of wood that makes certain sounds, but a mysterious vessel of divine realities. Music is the language of the spirit, but it comes to life through instruments. Music is a sacramental gift wherein the spiritual and the physical worlds unite. Often the instrument itself carries with it a storehouse of inspiration. The tones of a particular guitar or piano carry the artist into the birthing of a new song. Why? Because man is not merely a spiritual creature. Nor is he a mere animal. He is a sacramental creature—he has a physical and spiritual nature.

I have stumbled upon this reality as an actor many times: often the right emotion follows the right physicality. One of the best entryways into a scene is physical and not primarily emotional or intellectual. Countless times, the emotions are simply not present when I begin a scene; so I make the choice to inhabit a particular physicality appropriate to the character. Most of the time, the mind and emotions follow. As a musician, I find the right guitar tone can inspire a song that would never have been birthed otherwise. Something physical and tangible opens up a spiritual landscape.

Heaven and earth are not ultimately opposed to each other. Through the Incarnation of Christ and the grace of the Holy Spirit, the body is transformed into God's temple. In the prophetic context of the artist, he becomes a heavenly theater for the glory of God. After all, the Scriptures remind us: "Some have unwittingly entertained angels" (Heb. 13:2). (The reference here is to hospitality, but the concept could apply to the modern sense of entertainment as well.)

The study of the arts is an exploration into the very nature of man; and as Dostoevsky revealed in his novels, the paradoxical mystery of man can be uncovered only in the revelation of the God-Man, Jesus Christ. For the Christian, this is the true study of human nature, the true anthropology. The artist discovers himself "in Christ." He discovers the mystery of himself in the mystery of Christ because the Eternal Artist belongs to both heaven and earth. Through Christ, the artist returns to Eden. Once again, he becomes the sacrament he was created to be. The artist becomes truly human in beholding the face of Christ.

In the mystery of art and storytelling, something mystical takes place: Man, in all of his broken madness, is brought into the holy madness of Christ. Story is the fictional battlefield where we witness the unfolding drama of man's freedom and longing: his darkness and luminance: his fall and redemption. In our own lives, this cosmic encounter of light and darkness does not bring immediate serenity, but a conflict. It brings us into a struggle: a lifetime of epic choices, aspirations, and contradictions. Within this war of divisions, Christ is calling the artist back to unity and wholeness.

STEREOSCOPIC VISION: ACCEPTING THE ART OF PARADOX

Life is a paradox—and so is art. The most powerful moments in a song occur when the music and lyrics are pulling at each other with incredible tension. A part of the listener rises with hope, while the other part sinks into despair; and you don't know which one will triumph. It's the same with film: When great tragedy has occurred, but somehow the smallest glimmer of hope appears in the eyes of the hero, who has suffered so much—we can't help but be captivated and moved.

Poetry is unhindered paradox and contradiction. It seeks to communicate something mystically before that thing can be apprehended cognitively. It is the music of words. The spiritual life is the same; that is why St. Porphyrios said, "Whoever wants to become a Christian must first become a poet."[36] Poetry enables us to see things from more than one angle at the same time—just as in music, the miracle of counterpoint allows us to hear more than one melody at the same time. Somehow, when done right, it doesn't confuse us; it actually heightens the experience.

Creating in the Spirit requires stereoscopic vision. This

occurs in everyday life, in the natural course of using one's eyes. It is also an interesting analogy of the artistic life. Whenever we look at a particular object, we are using stereoscopic vision. Each eye views an object from a slightly different angle, so that if you close your left eye and open your right, the lamp in your room will appear in a certain place. But if you reverse this—closing your right eye while opening your left—the lamp will appear to have jumped or moved. Each eye is seeing the same object from a slightly different angle. When both of our eyes are open, looking at the same object, our brain takes the two different pictures and miraculously fuses them into one. Brilliant! This is a wonderful example of the paradox that exists in any true work of art. It is within the tension of contradiction that the flame of creativity is ignited and fanned.

St. Paul expressed this inner contradiction within the heart of humanity in the most personal of terms:

> For what I am doing, I do not understand. For what I will to do, that I do not practice; but what I hate, that I do. . . . For I know that in me (that is, in my flesh) nothing good dwells; for to will is present with me, but *how* to perform what is good I do not find. For the good that I will *to do*, I do not do; but the evil I will not *to do*, that I practice. Now if I do what I will not *to do*, it is no longer I who do it, but sin that dwells in me.
>
> I find then a law, that evil is present with me, the one who wills to do good. For I delight in the law of God according to the inward man. But I see another law in my members, war-

ring against the law of my mind, and bringing me into captivity to the law of sin which is in my members. O wretched
man that I am! Who will deliver me from this body of death?
(Rom. 7:15, 18-24)

This expresses the inner war of the human heart. The battlefield of desire, paradox, and contradiction is where the artist
finds himself, by virtue of his birth. He is born with an inner
turmoil as well as an inner light. He finds himself on the front
lines, so to speak, of humanity's spiritual plight, acutely aware
of his mortality. And yet eternity is burning bright within him.
The acceptance of paradox and contradiction is vital to the
honesty of any artist. This is why fundamentalist Christianity
is so damaging to the culture—it does not have the ability to
see paradox or humility.

The Trinity is a transcendent paradox. By virtue of being
made in the image of God, humanity is also paradoxical. We
are utterly mysterious and sacramental. Without intimate
knowledge of the paradoxical God, the artist will remain in
chaos within himself, looking for answers that only bear the
Name of a multifaceted Person—Jesus Christ. We are complex
beings, seeking (even starving) for inner harmony: a holistic
salvation, in which all the senses are redeemed and healed.
Embracing paradox allows the artist to reflect humanity's
struggles as well as our divine calling.

SPIRITUAL AND PHYSICAL UNION: AWAKENING THE FIVE SENSES

The artist seeks to participate in a holistic revelation of life. This takes more than analytical research. It takes the spiritual engagement of the entire person. Our inspiration for this is found in the Scriptures themselves—primarily from two revelations. The prophet Isaiah and St. John the Theologian were both given visions of heaven and the worship taking place there.

Here is Isaiah's account:

> In the year that King Uzziah died, I saw the Lord sitting on a throne, high and lifted up, and the train of His *robe* filled the temple. Above it stood seraphim; each one had six wings: with two he covered his face, with two he covered his feet, and with two he flew. And one cried to another and said:
> "Holy, holy, holy *is* the Lord of hosts;
> The whole earth *is* full of His glory!"
> And the posts of the door were shaken by the voice of him who cried out, and the house was filled with smoke.
> So I said:
> "Woe *is* me, for I am undone!
> Because I *am* a man of unclean lips,
> And I dwell in the midst of a people of unclean lips;
> For my eyes have seen the King,
> The Lord of hosts."
> Then one of the seraphim flew to me, having in his hand a live coal *which* he had taken with the tongs from the altar. And he touched my mouth *with it*, and said:

"Behold, this has touched your lips;
Your iniquity is taken away,
And your sin purged." (Is. 6:1–7)

Isaiah saw the Lord; he heard the angels saying "Holy, holy, holy"; he felt the foundations shake beneath and around him; smoke filled the house like incense, whereby he could smell the prayers swirling around him; and finally, he tastes the mercy of God when the seraph touches his mouth and says, "Your guilt is taken away" (a foreshadowing of the Eucharist). This vision is in perfect harmony with that of St. John in the Book of Revelation. These prophetic accounts of heaven are essential to the artist who knows he is made in the Image of God. He is called to bring heaven down to earth. If that is true, then it behooves him to know a little of what heaven is like.

In heaven, we hear the word of God, we see the face of God (in Christ), we feel the power of the indwelling Spirit of God, we smell the holy incense as it rises upward, and we taste the goodness of God in the Mystery of Holy Communion. The whole man is engaged in this relational dynamism.

With this as the artist's foundation and ethos, the sky opens up before him. He begins to climb the ladder of divine ascent both spiritually and artistically.

All the senses are united in a cosmic mystery of grace. The artist loses sight of his ego and himself. These are the moments of emptiness in which he is truly filled to overflowing. He is caught up in the fire of the moment, or rather, caught up in the fire of the One who possesses the moment he is in. It is in these mystical moments that the artist learns the art of ascension—the art of flying. Everything up until this point remains abstract. It is in the fire of revelation and experience that he becomes an actual artist.

His entire being is engaged: "You shall love the Lord your God with all your heart, with all your soul, with all your strength, and with all your mind,' and 'your neighbor as yourself'" (Luke 10:27). The artist's existence is holistic. It begins with the heart, inhabits his entire soul, traverses into the very fabric and sinews of his body (his strength), and sets up a home in his mind. He knows that he cannot love God with his mind alone, and he cannot be the artist he was created to be through his intellectual capacities alone. The artist's entire being is awakened in the pursuit of love. He is embracing the fullness of life. The artist engages the heart in the depths of his soul and embraces the physical world as a sacrament of God.

When the artist contemplates this mystery, he will soon realize his faith cannot be rooted in judgment or oppression. It must be rooted in the freedom of man. There is no coercion in the heart of heaven. Christ would rather suffer crucifixion than take away the freedom of man. Bringing heaven to earth means loving the world without any lust for power or dominion over others. It is to be saturated in the freedom of love and the love of freedom.

The artist is no longer the slave of men but a child of the Father of Lights. " And whatever you do, do it heartily, as to the Lord and not to men" (Col. 3:23). Every moment is significant; every day holds the presence of eternity. In his joy, the artist continuously prays, "Your kingdom come, Your will be done, on earth as it is in heaven" (Matt. 6:10).

INDIVIDUALISM OR A THEOPHANY OF BEAUTY

Our society is inflicted with two opposing political worldviews: the capitalistic emphasis on the rights of the individual and the socialistic belief in the virtues of collectivism. On the one hand, there is the Marxist counterfeit to the Christian Gospel: collectivism. This ideology preaches unity at the expense of man's freedom and devalues the uniqueness of each person. The Gospel envisions humanity as being created in the image of God in order to become "one" in Christ, while never losing the uniqueness of each person in the process.

On the other hand, there is the capitalistic counterfeit of materialism, which promotes an extreme individualism that justifies greed and self-centeredness in the name of freedom. The Gospel upholds the freedom of man and the unique beauty of each soul, but it also condemns self-centeredness, materialism, and apathy toward the poor. It condemns the modern notion of individualism.

Other than a belief in a vague form of social justice, capitalism has almost no understanding of humans being cosmically connected to one another. Everything points toward the self: iPhone, iPad, iPod, Facebook . . . I, I, I, me, me, me. This is the state of our culture. The selling point is that these technologies will help people stay connected to each other, but in reality, they often separate people from authentic relationships. Teenagers become addicted to texting, to the point that they are incapable of eating dinner or watching a movie without continuously checking their smartphones.

Despite, or because of, all the incredible technology our society has at its fingertips, human beings are becoming more and more isolated. Suicide, drug abuse, and depression continue to increase. To make up for our inability to love one another in totality, society elevates social causes to ease our consciences. Human beings are losing the ability to actually love each other, even as they are heroically taking on huge social problems throughout the world. The words of St. Paul the Apostle come to mind: "And though I bestow all my goods to feed *the poor*, and though I give my body to be burned, but have not love, it profits me nothing" (1 Cor. 13:3).

Amidst these opposing worldviews and ideologies, traditional Christianity embodies the paradoxical healing of the Gospel of Jesus Christ. This Gospel at once upholds the value and uniqueness of the person, and the cosmic unity of all things in Christ. It supports the worthy social causes of the world, but always emphasizes their deepest purpose, which is to truly love one another. It defends the rights of the individual because every human being is created in the image of God and has intrinsic value. It embraces the world, not materialistically or politically, but sacramentally.

One of the most profound examples of this sacramental power in the liturgical life of Eastern Christianity is the Feast of the Theophany of Our Lord. This liturgical event expresses the cosmic healing of all creation. It beautifully proclaims that in Christ, the whole world is once again a sacrament.

In this feast, the *ecclesia* (the assembly) not only celebrates and remembers the Baptism of Christ, but actually participates in the grace of this sacred event. It is a timeless reality. Somehow, through the grace of the Holy Spirit, the Church is present at the Jordan River, mystically experiencing this holy occasion. The joy of this feast is so great that the church cannot remain within her own walls. She has to gather outside, in the sanctuary of nature, at a river or a lake for the Great Blessing of Water.

According to the Fathers of Christianity, when Christ was baptized in the Jordan River, the whole of creation was sanctified and made new—not merely the waters of the Jordan, but the whole of creation. The entire world is made new in the Theophany of Christ. It is not an isolated, individualistic salvation—it belongs to every human being, the world, and the universe itself. It is not only the faithful present within the walls of the church (or gathered around a river) who receive sanctification and healing on this great feast, but the whole world. It is a mystery too glorious to be contained by time and space. The Church, with authority, speaks in the present tense: "Today!" The Theophany of Our Lord takes place. How can she proclaim this? The Church proclaims this because she belongs to the eternal life of the Trinity. She is not bound by time.

The priest often reads the Theophany poem of Sophronios, Patriarch of Jerusalem, during the service. This poetic prayer expresses the sacramental wonder of the Church and its cosmic vision of redemption. This is the mystery the artist is invited to partake in.

> For today the time for feasting has come and the choir of the saints holds assembly with us, and angels celebrate with men. Today the grace of the Holy Spirit, in the form of a dove, came upon the waters. Today the unwaning sun has dawned, and the world is lit up with the light of the Lord. Today the moon with its brilliant rays shares its light with the earth. Today the luminous stars embellish the universe with their joyous luster. Today the clouds refresh humanity with a rain of justice from above. Today the uncreated One is by His own will touched by the creature. Today the prophet and forerunner approaches the Master, but pauses in awe, seeing God's condescension towards us.
>
> Today the waters of the Jordan are turned into healing by the presence of the Lord. Today all creation is watered by mystical waters. Today men's sins are washed away in the waters of the Jordan. Today Paradise is thrown open to humankind, and the sun of righteousness shines upon us. Today the water that the people under Moses found bitter is turned into sweetness at the Lord's presence. . . .
>
> The waters saw You, O God, the waters saw You and were afraid. . . . The Jordan turned back and the mountains leapt, seeing God in the flesh, and the clouds gave voice, marveling at the One present, light of light, true God of true God, Who submerged in the Jordan the death of disobedience and the sting of error and the bond of Hades, giving to the world a baptism of salvation.

Ode to a Spiritual Warrior

Though no sword thy hand ever wielded or raised,
Great multitudes hast thou slain.
On bended knee with eyes both strident and gazed,
Thy words were arrows aflame.

Thou didst walk through life with mercy as thy steel
And love thy wakening bell.
"Arise, Precious Soul," thy heart would oft appeal
To a hidden, unseen realm.

Amidst the darkness, thy spirit hath prevailed,
Prizing truth above the din,
Giving grace to light the captive bound and jailed
In shadowy walls of sin.

No field so wretched as the bloodied winter
With pools of scarlet mourning,
Where conceit doth bind the eye to the splinter
And grudge allay the warning.

Though Achilles' strength trumpets sound and fury
In one prayer, more hast thou done,
For temporal praise wilts as time doth scurry,
But peace thy heart hath won.

Though fleshly commands surrender to the days,
Still inward thy might doth grow.
For every battle waged in love's countless ways
Hath increased thy wisdom's glow.

So thou journeyest, across perilous sea,
Guarded by faith's unseen sword,
Joining the chorus of heaven's blissful plea
Until thou dost meet Love's reward.

8

ART AS

Offering

*And the light shines in the darkness,
and the darkness did not comprehend it.*

JOHN 1:5

It is quite easy for artists to look at their careers as an invest-ment. They work this hard, invest this much time, energy, and commitment, and it seems only logical they should reap the empirical benefits at some reasonable date. They get caught up in the concept of success and so easily lose sight of the jour-ney and the process of life.

A friend of mine, who is also an artist, once told me, "I'm learning that each day is an offering, not an investment." What a beautiful thought: to let go of the outcomes in life and receive the beauty of the journey, the peace of the moment. A saint once said, "This moment is the most important moment of your entire life." Why? Because it is the only moment one truly possesses. This moment, right now, is alive to us. Salvation is to be found here, in communion with God. Every day is an offering, a reason for praise and exaltation. Every morning is a foreshadowing of the resurrection that is to come.

THE ART OF CHRONOS & KAIROS: AN OFFERING IN TIME

The ancient Greeks had two words to describe time: *chronos* and *kairos*. Chronos is where the word *chronology* comes from. It means sequential time: the passing of time. Kairos means the appointed time or the crisis. The cosmic opportunity. The eternal moment. The supreme moment! As the Divine Liturgy is about to commence, the deacon says to the priest, *"Kairos tou poiesai to Kyrio"* ("It is time [kairos] for the Lord to act"). The time of the Liturgy enters into the realm of eternity. The artist is meant to become a liturgical being; his entire life is meant to be an intersection with eternity: a kairos.

Throughout Scripture we find continual reference to the present moment. The first words of Christ's earthly ministry were, "Repent, for the kingdom of heaven is at hand" (Matt. 3:2). The kingdom of heaven is near. The Hebrew word *karav* gives an even more immediate interpretation: The kingdom of heaven is here. It is now. The artist is called to break through the constraints of man's chronology, breathe immortal life into the mundaneness of existence, and make an eternal offering in time.

Christ says, "The time [kairos] is fulfilled, and the kingdom of God is at hand. Repent, and believe in the gospel" (Mark 1:15). When He taught His disciples to pray, He said, "Give us this day our daily bread" (Matt. 6:11), enjoining us to remain in the present moment. He also said:

> "Therefore I say to you, do not worry about your life, what you will eat or what you will drink; nor about your body, what you will put on. Is not life more than food and the body more than clothing? Look at the birds of the air, for they neither sow nor reap nor gather into barns; yet your heavenly Father feeds them. Are you not of more value than they? Which of you by worrying can add one cubit to his stature?
>
> "So why do you worry about clothing? Consider the lilies of the field, how they grow: they neither toil nor spin; and yet I say to you that even Solomon in all his glory was not arrayed like one of these. Now if God so clothes the grass of the field, which today is, and tomorrow is thrown into the oven, *will He* not much more *clothe* you, O you of little faith?
>
> "Therefore do not worry, saying, 'What shall we eat?' or 'What shall we drink?' or 'What shall we wear?' For after all these things the Gentiles seek. For your heavenly Father knows that you need all these things. But seek first the kingdom of God and His righteousness, and all these things shall be added to you. Therefore do not worry about tomorrow, for tomorrow will worry about its own things. Sufficient for the day is its own trouble." (Matt. 6:25–34)

In times of coming crisis, Christ exhorted His disciples by saying, "But when they deliver you up, do not worry about how or what you should speak. For it will be given to you *in that hour* what you should speak; for it is not you who speak, but the Spirit of your Father who speaks in you" (Matt. 10:19–20, emphasis added).

The Apostle Paul expressed the kairos of Christ's Incarnation and Crucifixion thus: "For when we were still without strength, in due time [kairos] Christ died for the ungodly" (Rom. 5:6). This expresses the historical event that took place. In between chronos, kairos intervened and took action. But how does this event change the reality of time? St. Paul continues his theme on kairos, but a profound transition takes place from the historical event of the Cross to its relevance in the ongoing life of man: "praying always [lit., "at all *kairoi*"] with all prayer and supplication in the Spirit, being watchful to this end with all perseverance and supplication for all the saints" (Eph. 6:18).

It is a transition into the language of the Spirit. The Cross has altered man's relationship with God forever. Therefore, kairos, the appointed time, the time of crisis, the supreme moment, becomes available to humanity now. The artist is an instrument of this grace for the life of the world.

Again, St. Paul the Apostle instructs, "Rejoice always, pray without ceasing, in everything give thanks; for this is the will of God in Christ Jesus for you" (1 Thess. 5:16–18). Pray now, in this moment. Do not wait for tomorrow to experience grace—to become like Christ. The appointed time is *now*.

The Holy Spirit has come. The world has been changed and transformed. Tongues of fire have been poured out on those who believe and are baptized into Christ. The eternal now is with us. Emmanuel—God is with us. Now, we pray, "O Heavenly King, Comforter, Spirit of Truth, who are everywhere present and fill all things." The Book of Hebrews speaks about the Sabbath as an appointed day, sanctified to be holy. But it also speaks of another day that has been sanctified.

> For He has spoken in a certain place of the seventh *day* in this way: "And God rested on the seventh day from all His works"; and again in this *place*: "They shall not enter My rest."
> Since therefore it remains that some *must* enter it, and those to whom it was first preached did not enter because of disobedience, again He designates a certain day, saying in David, "Today," after such a long time, as it has been said:
> "Today, if you will hear His voice,
> Do not harden your hearts." (Heb. 4:4–7)

Orthodox Christianity speaks in the language of the eternal now. On Great and Holy Friday the Church proclaims:

> *Today* He who hung the land in the midst of the waters is hung upon the Tree. A crown of thorns crowns Him who is King of angels. He who wrapped the heavens with clouds is wrapped about with the purple of mockery. He who freed Adam in Jordan received buffetings. He who is the Bridegroom of the Church was transfixed with nails. He who is the Son of the Virgin was pierced with a spear. We worship Your Passion, O Christ. Show also unto us Your glorious Resurrection.

On Holy Saturday she proclaims:

> *Today* a tomb holds Him who holds the creation in the hollow of His hand; a stone covers Him who covered the heavens with glory. Life sleeps and hell trembles, and Adam is set free from his bonds. Glory to Your dispensation, whereby You have accomplished all things, granting us an eternal Sabbath, Your most holy Resurrection from the dead.

On Pascha she proclaims, "*Today* all creation is glad and rejoices, for Christ has risen and hell has been conquered." "Christ is risen from the dead, trampling down death by death, and upon those in the tombs bestowing life!"

The Church does not simply remember that two thousand years ago Christ rose from the dead, but she says, "Christ *is* risen!" in the present tense. The Church is cosmically linked to that event through the presence of the Holy Spirit. The event of the Resurrection is both within and outside of time. It is a part of chronos and kairos. The Book of Revelation refers to "the Lamb slain from the foundation of the world" (Rev. 13:8).

Pentecost was the manifestation of the Church in the world. But the Fathers teach that the Church existed in the reality of God from eternity. Christ came to give us back the eternal moment that Adam and Eve possessed before the Fall. Christ comes and says, "The kingdom of God is within you" (Luke 17:21). This moment has become the most important moment of your life. It is a supreme moment.

The Church has given the artist a profound spiritual

weapon in the Jesus prayer—the prayer of the heart: "Lord Jesus Christ, Son of God, have mercy on me, a sinner." The appointed time to pray the Jesus prayer is *always*. Notice how the Apostle Paul joins "pray without ceasing" with "Rejoice always!" Prayer and rejoicing are one act. The prayer of the heart helps the artist to abide in the presence of Christ. It helps him to remain in the eternal moment of creation.

By invoking the Name above all names, acknowledging his lordship over our lives and humbly petitioning His mercy, the artist enters into communion with Him. In Greek, the word for *mercy* has the same root as the word for *oil*, which is a symbol of the Holy Spirit. When the artist prays this prayer, he is asking Christ to pour out the Holy Spirit upon him and heal him.

This is how the artist begins to understand what it means to be in the world but not of it. To be in the world means that the Christian lives, breathes, and functions in chronos—in a timeline, so to speak. He is bound by this empirical reality. He is in the world. But he is not of the world. He exists in kairos—the appointed time, the mystical "today." The Jesus prayer brings the heart into union with this eternal reality. The artist is always in the eternal now of transformation. He is being developed. Salvation is happening right now. St. Isaac the Syrian said, "This life was given to you for repentance; do not waste it in vain pursuits."[37] Every step of the way, chronos is unfolding and kairos is present in the form of grace and invitation. The eternal present, the kingdom of heaven, is within you.

IT'S ALWAYS TEN THOUSAND

When union with God is the artist's highest desire and pursuit, the world can no longer demoralize him. When he sees his life and his work as an offering instead of an investment, he is free from the enslavement of man's approval. He is able to approach any outcome with the peace of the Jesus prayer. In the brilliant book *The Mountain of Silence*, Fr. Maximos expresses this liberation: "Remember, whatever good or bad things happen to us, they have only one single purpose, to awaken us to the reality of God and help us on the path toward union with Him. There is no other reason for being born on this planet, believe me. It is up to us whether or not we take advantage of these wake-up calls."[38] Whether suffering or consolation, pain or joy, mourning or rejoicing, each moment is an invitation to become transformed within into the likeness of Christ and to experience His transcendent joy.

The worldly constructs of success and failure become foreign and inconsequential to the soul who is seeking first "the kingdom of God and His righteousness" (Matt. 6:33). Success is redefined as abiding in God; failure would be to lose hope or to choose to become a self-worshiping narcissist. Whether or not one's career takes off is irrelevant.

A particularly powerful moment in my journey happened when I was performing a concert with my band Enation, many years ago. We had been working very hard for a few years to get our music heard: fifteen-hour drives in a van, months in the studio recording, investing our own money into the dream, and believing with our whole hearts that we would soon see a payoff. We thought we were investing! We booked a few shows, and for some reason, no one was really turning up. Promotion was nonexistent, and it felt like a huge waste of time, money, and energy. On this particular night there were only about ten people in the club where we were performing, and probably seven of them were friends and family.

The important thing about the story is that we didn't allow circumstances to drag us down into discouragement or despair. We went out there and put on a show that literally felt like we were in a stadium. It was powerful. Practically no one saw it. But it didn't really matter to me for some reason. I knew we had put on an amazing show and perhaps even "unwittingly entertained angels" (Heb. 13:2).

There's a common saying among bands playing in front of small numbers of people: "Ten or ten thousand." Meaning, you go out and perform whether it's in front of ten or ten thousand people. But after this particular night, I knew it was always ten thousand, because the angels of God were present, regardless of how many people showed up. This was a big turning point for me. Success wasn't to be measured by human standards.

Artists do not receive glory from people; they live in the secret glory of their Father. This makes them strange to the world—but it also frees them to love the world from the reality of heaven.

ART AS SPIRITUAL WARFARE

If one is called to be a professional artist, then he has been sent as a specific light to a specific darkness (it is the same for everyone, in the uniqueness of their vocation). The spiritual warfare the artist encounters will be varied and complex. Rejection and disappointment will likely be a significant part of his journey. Criticism and judgment will be commonplace. Competition will be ruthless. Some will love the peace they sense in him; others will be offended that he doesn't bow before the idols of anxiety, fame, greed, and success. But in all this warfare, love overcomes every human instinct of fear.

Many people refer to the entertainment industry as Babylon, and there are some understandable reasons for this. The intense love of money and lust for power is quite obvious. But there are so many beautiful and inspiring people in this creative industry: this should never be lost on the artist. Christ loves the people in Hollywood. I, for one, enjoy having genuine friendships with people who disagree with me. I love seeing the beauty in them and learning from their humility, creativity, and gifts. Christ is in them: How could I not be in awe of who they are?

This does not make one stupid—just innocent. Thus, another paradox Christ lays out before the artist: "Be wise as serpents and harmless [or innocent] as doves" (Matt. 10:16). This means that as the artist walks in the Spirit, he becomes capable of engaging in spiritual warfare successfully.

To engage in this conflict successfully means that his love for people never diminishes. In fact, it should always be increasing. This is a delicate but vitally important spiritual endeavor. The Apostle Paul revealed this distinction to us:

> For we do not wrestle against flesh and blood, but against principalities, against powers, against the rulers of the darkness of this age, against spiritual *hosts* of wickedness in the heavenly *places*. (Eph. 6:12)

The artist does not go to war against people. But he does fight against the spiritual forces of evil in the heavenly places, and he does this with all his strength. It is enlightening to know that our spiritual preparation for a performance does not simply revolve around the performance itself. There is a spiritual drama taking place all around us, and creating in the Spirit involves this awareness. This means, for instance, that the artist learns how to maintain inner peace while inhabiting a dynamic reality for his performance.

One example of spiritual warfare is acting in romantic situations. It's a fair example of this tightrope and a controversial one. As an actor, one enters into the fictional reality of the romance—but the actor is never to be taken over by this fiction. He is aware of the spiritual warfare going on around him, and this keeps him vigilant and watchful. All of these boundaries are easily crossed if Christ is not consciously living within at least one of the two performers. There are so many examples of this that it's unnecessary to give any here; we are all too aware of them from the covers of magazines at grocery stores.

But romantic situations are only one example of the spiritual warfare that often occurs. It can also manifest in extremely difficult relationships with various people in any artistic medium. Creative individuals tend to be passionate, and this lends itself to explosive situations and personalities. Learning how to reside in peace and exhibit the patience, confidence, and humility of Christ is an ongoing pursuit. And it is a worthy goal that can be attained only through the grace of the Holy Spirit.

It may seem strange to portray events and characters that are not holy and beautiful or to write songs about troubled souls. But, in reality, it is not strange at all. Who better to prophetically enter into the depths of humanity than those who are living in ceaseless prayer with God? It is as strange as Dostoevsky writing *Crime and Punishment, Demons, Notes from the Underground, Memoirs from the House of the Dead,* or *The Brothers Karamazov.* This creative engagement can only occur with a deep love for mankind. That's the brilliance of Christ: His holiness increases our love for man. It never diminishes it through shallow self-righteousness. The holiness of Christ brings us closer to humanity: closer to our true beauty and fearsome darkness. Any talk of Christianity that displays a haughty distance toward the brokenness and vulnerability of humanity has nothing to do with Christ.

He is the Divine Son who wept at the grave of Lazarus, rejoiced at the wedding in Cana, forgave the woman caught in adultery, sweated blood in the Garden of Gethsemane, and prayed for forgiveness over those who were having Him crucified. (Cosmically speaking, that would be each one of us, through our blindness to love.)

God is close to man's internal war, because it is here, in the heart of man, where the gift of freedom resides. Spiritual warfare is ultimately experienced within the heart of man. This is where light and darkness dwell (where the artist should dwell) in the epicenter of man's freedom. It is "in the liberty by which Christ has made us free" (Gal. 5:1).

The artist can also (albeit with caution) enter into the spiritual warfare of the story, poem, or character he is approaching. There are times when a character is experiencing various accusations from the enemy of God, and in these instances the artist may be called to prophetically suffer under these lies, portraying the intense brokenness and fear of mankind.

The artist is called to "rejoice with those who rejoice, and weep with those who weep" (Rom. 12:15). Knowing a character's greatest fear is as important as knowing his or her greatest desire. Again, it is essential for the artist to be wise in this spiritual and creative discourse. The artist is giving voice prophetically to the struggles and triumphs of humanity. Therefore, every form of art is at all times a kind of spiritual warfare. This is important to remember because spiritual warfare does not vanish when one forgets about it. One just becomes a passive victim to it.

ART AND ASCETICISM

There is a fascinating connection between art and asceticism, which Fr. Thomas Hopko has shed light on. It may seem a bit abstract at first, but it is crucially important to the creative life. Asceticism essentially means discipline, exercise, or training. In the footnotes of *When Hearts Become Flame*, Stephen Muse expressed it this way: "Asceticism rightly understood is the struggle to become free of lesser forces in order to be responsive to the greater force of grace."[39]

A person abstains for a time from things morally neutral or even good (like food or nuptial intimacy) for the sake of being awakened to their true beauty and goodness. This also awakens the awareness of his need for and dependence on God.

As the Fathers of the Church teach, asceticism is a means to an end—not an end in itself. In keeping with this tradition, Fr. Hopko reflected that if a person were to completely neglect any self-denial in his life, he would become an animal, following only his carnal instincts. If, however, he abused spiritual disciplines and used them as tools of self-righteousness to puff himself up in his own eyes (using them as an end in themselves), then he would become a demon. This is an even worse form of existence than that of a mere animal. Asceticism is necessary, but only as a means to another end.[40] Namely, the "acquisition of the Holy Spirit," as St. Seraphim of Sarov taught.

The aim of asceticism is for the person to dwell in the Holy Spirit, where true freedom resides. This freedom will give him the grace to love in greater union with the Divine. Fasting and other healthy ascetic disciplines are not obligations. Rather, they are tools the artist can use to grow in intimacy with God, if they are approached with humility and balance, under the guidance of a spiritual father.

An intriguing situation is recorded in the Gospels in which Christ's disciples could not cast a demon out of someone. They had attempted this before and had been successful, so they were confused. They asked Jesus why they couldn't do it this time. He responded, "This kind can come out by nothing but prayer and fasting" (Mark 9:29). This reveals a genuine connection between spiritual authority and living lives of asceticism.

In the realm of spiritual warfare, it is necessary for the artist to remain sharp, watchful, vigilant, awake, and sensitive to the Spirit of God. These ascetical tools for training help him along the journey. When we approach these exercises and disciplines, not in our own strength, but in the grace of God, they assist us in our ability to pray with Christ, "nevertheless, not what I will, but what You *will*" (Mark 14:36). This kenosis or emptying of self is a lifelong process of struggle. Many saints refer to this process as *deification* or *theosis*.

Asceticism allows the artist to be lovingly chiseled by the Holy Spirit as he himself chisels away at his craft or performance. Again, Fr. Hopko states, "Human persons create genuine works of art only when they are themselves works of art."[41]

This is the desire of the artist. He desires not only to produce dynamic performances and works of art that reflect the deepest parts of humanity, but also to produce a dynamic life that reflects eternal realities—the latter being the most important aspiration.

Emptying himself of his many delusions and false identities equips the artist to receive the creative force of the Spirit in greater depth. It helps him to receive another vision than merely his own and gives him the boldness to follow it through, even if this vision challenges his preconceptions or natural limitations.

Every situation in life comes down to emptying oneself (kenosis) and becoming alive to the greater force of grace.

Marriage, for example, is an incredible form of asceticism: one is daily called to lay down his or her own desires for the sake of the beloved. Raising children is another magnificent form of asceticism. You cannot remain a self-centered artist if you wish to raise your children with dedication and intentionality. You will have to die to your own desires and resurrect to the desires of an unconditionally loving God. Everything in life—our work, dreams, relationships, triumphs and trials—are all given to us so that we might become alive to the beauty and mystery of Christ's love.

The artist's response to each of these ascetical circumstances in life unites with one of the most powerful ascetics in history, John the Baptist: "[Christ] must increase, but I *must decrease*" (John 3:30). This is the life of the artist. *Jesus Christ must increase, but I must decrease.* This vision does not lead him into nirvana, a state of nothingness. It leads him into a state of true personhood, uniqueness, and dynamism as a child of God. This vision allows the artist to embrace all of humanity and the entire world. He loses sight of his lower life in order to gain the invaluable gift of his higher life.

The focus of our spiritual struggle should never be on what we are letting go of or losing, but on what we are gaining: "love, joy, peace, longsuffering, kindness, goodness, faithfulness, gentleness, self-control" (Gal. 5:22–23). The spiritual life is not about what one heroically gives to God, but what he is willing to receive from Him. As Archimandrite Aimilianos of Simonopetra said, "Communion with God is a constant receiving from God, and not a giving of anything to Him."[42] Elsewhere, he described what this process is like:

> I begin to feel the joy of a small child who has found his
> father, after believing that he'd lost him forever. Having found
> his father, the child claps his hands, laughs, and shouts for
> joy. So too do we experience primordial joy when we discover
> that, like Adam in paradise, we are walking with God. The
> soul now lives as if every day it were celebrating a feast. Such a
> soul becomes festal, celebratory, joyous. It acquires a different
> kind of piety, based on its experiences, and which is conse-
> quently more powerful, more authentic.[43]

The smallest glimpse of God's love makes everything in this world appear like a mere shadow compared to the blazing sun. Asceticism is not about what one is abstaining from, but what he is saying yes to. As Fr. Stephen Rogers, rector of Holy Trinity Church in Franklin, Tennessee, says, "Asceticism is an emptying to create the space to be filled. A vessel that is full cannot make room for anything else." The artist is invited to say goodbye to those things that keep him oppressed: his fears, delusions, pride, anger, self-righteousness, and so on.

If he lives a life of daily surrender, trust, and transcendence, death will not hurt as much in the end. "O death, where is your sting?" (1 Cor. 15:55). Asceticism is learning how to say good-bye to the shadowy things of life and fully embrace the eternal realities: the love of God, His children, and His creation.

Throughout life, the spiritual artist is able to embrace thousands and thousands of mini-deaths so that in the end, whenever that may be, he can approach his death without being a slave to fear.

> Inasmuch then as the children have partaken flesh and
> blood, He Himself likewise shared in the same, that through
> death He might destroy him who had the power of death,
> that is, the devil, and release those who through fear of death
> were all their lifetime subject to bondage. (Heb. 2:14–15)

It is Christ who frees man from this fear and darkness. And perhaps the greatest darkness one will ever experience on this earth is within his heart. This is why a life of prayer, fasting, worship, and almsgiving (all done for Christ's sake) is so important, because it relates to the eternal reality of man's ever-deepening union with the Holy Trinity.

There is an external cosmic war taking place. But the internal cosmic war is what the artist is most concerned with. He is invited to uncover the light within the darkness of his own soul, so that he may truly become one of the lights of the world: a light the darkness cannot overcome.

9

‒‒‒◆‒‒‒

Rejoice, O Artists

"These things I have spoken to you, that My joy may remain in you, and that your joy may be full."

JOHN 15:11

I was about to turn nineteen years old, and up until that point in my career, I had mostly played dark roles: a Northern Irish suicidal teenager, a heroin addict, the leader of a fringe militia, an abusive boyfriend, and a serial killer. These were among the roles I found myself portraying at a young age. Landing the role of Jessie Tuck in *Tuck Everlasting* was such a blessing. He was a character of immense enthusiasm for life and a natural disposition of joy. It was refreshing to harmonize the joy of knowing Christ with the innocence and exuberance this character was supposed to possess.

Performing those scenes actually uplifted my own faith in the beauty and goodness of God. I saw this character as another symbol of Christ: he had drunk from the fountain of immortality and could no longer die nor age. Jessie received this unexplainable circumstance as a miracle worth rejoicing in. I made the choice as an actor that Jessie's joy was not an accident; he had made a clear choice at some point in his life (he had already lived for more than a hundred years) to remain joyful, grateful, and innocent. I felt this would give his presence more weight and authority, and that his words and expressions would ultimately be more complex and captivating.

Jessie fell in love with Winnie Foster and opened up a whole new world of possibilities and horizons for her. Her world was drab, conformed, joyless, and oppressive. His was wild, spontaneous, and liberating. I couldn't help but see an allegory of Christ as the Eternal One, inviting humanity into a sacred romance of mystery and adventure. It was a blessing to portray that story: at its heart was a hymn of rejoicing.

So how does joy relate to the life of the artist? What does its presence mean? One cannot venture far into the deep waters of the creative life without continually being transformed and refreshed by the inspiration of joy. Every artist becomes infused with joy about his or her artistic pursuit—whether it is music, poetry, acting, directing, painting, sculpting, writing, dancing, or any other expression. The artist is overwhelmed by the joy of this mystery. But with this exuberance comes the inevitable suffering at the very hands of one's passion.

Van Gogh, for instance, fell in love with painting. It infused him with immense energy and profound joy. However, it soon became an obsession he could not rid himself of. There was a particular golden yellow color the brilliant painter experimented with over and over again: it enveloped his every thought. He simply could not get enough of his passionate artistic pursuit.

In the end, Van Gogh's creative fire did not fulfill the deepest longings of his heart. His temporal joy and creative ecstasy could not quench his cosmic yearning. It eventually turned into bitter sorrow, ending in suicide. This is a tragic and timeless portrait of an artist who gives his heart to the momentary joy of his craft but loses sight of his eternal joy: communion with God.

God has given incredible gifts to His children, but what happens to the artist when he falls in love with the gifts of creation instead of the Giver of Life? The gifts, which are beautiful in and of themselves, betray his heart and leave him unfulfilled and lost. There are two kinds of spiritual and creative fire. One fire brings temporary joy (or happiness) but eventually leads to sorrow and death. The other kind of fire is divine communion, which is everlasting and unquenchable joy. This fire burns and wounds initially, but eventually leads to ecstasy and everlasting life.

The aspiration of this book is the reorientation of the artist back to the eternal essence of his nature. To inspire an attraction toward that fire that burns not to destroy, but to purify the heart by giving it the strength of the phoenix, which rises from the temporal ashes of this world toward its heavenly destiny. The joy of the Trinity is a burning fire: something unspeakably beautiful and hauntingly transcendent. One word to describe this indescribable reality is *joy*. This word has unfortunately been watered down by our society. It must be rediscovered in the light of the Kingdom of heaven. The spiritual power of divine joy is essential to the creative force of the artist. Joy is the interior disposition counter to narcissism.

Before we continue further, here is a strange little prose poem on the subject of the inadequacy of words:

The apocalyptic poet mused, "Art is useless if it does not assist in the recovery of wonder."

The attentive toad who was sitting nearby replied, with a degree of worldly pomp, "Elysian sentiments, my errant human, only dull the intellect to the factual truths of consequentialism."

The poet responded, "If mystery were to suffer an absolute death, so would the very hearts of men."

The toad looked out into the boring water. "Well, perhaps that is the difference between men and toads. Good day to you, young poet." The toad hopped away on a lily pad of placid monotony.

"Good day to you, as well," the poet responded with a curious countenance.

If only there were more words, he thought. *What word might I use to express or allude to this feeling of magic? Any word my soul brings forth seems only to limit and imprison this feeling. Where am I to turn, if not to words?*

And then the Voice spoke, as the Voice often does to

poets and prophets alike, "The word does not limit the feeling; the feeling expands the word."

Book of Silence and the Subconscious Awe

The word (*joy*) will not limit our discovery. Rather, it is our discovery that will expand the word. The Greek word for joy is *chairo*. This word is related to *charis*, which means "grace." Joy, therefore, is literally rooted in grace. Every time we experience a revelation of grace, joy is the natural consequence. If joy is lacking in a man's heart (or perhaps even limping), there is a revelation of grace awaiting him.

Another word connected to joy is *rejoice*. It is basically the same word, only in action. To live in joy is to rejoice! St. Paul could say, "Rejoice in the Lord always" (Phil. 4:4) precisely because of the reality of grace. "Rejoice in the Lord always"—because He is always rejoicing in you.

The artist is not merely speaking words—after all, words are only shadows and indications of what one experiences with God. She is contemplating something otherworldly. Every transcendent delight of this age—romance, having children, witnessing a beautiful sunset, and so on—is only a shadow of an eternal joy.

Joy is ultimately supernatural. It is not in the artist's power to manufacture. Divine joy is not simply another virtue. It is not an equal opposite to sorrow. It is not an equal opposite to anything. It is what Christ is to the devil. It has no equal. Joy is the very language of heaven: C. S. Lewis wittingly said, "Joy is the serious business of heaven."[44] Joy is higher, deeper, broader, and infinitely more profound than the natural realm. It is more intense than sorrow. It is literally stronger. It is dominant and more forceful. It is more passionate than pain or discouragement. There is more within it; in its substance. It is literally a stronger energy force—because it is the energy of God.

The fallen human condition is one of constant reaction to the winds of circumstance. It permits man to be tossed to and fro by the myriad waves and troubles of this life. He is constantly susceptible to fear, envy, anger, and depression. Man is like the moon in this fallen state: filled with craters and darkness, cold and barren—and on his best day he radiates a soft glow of hope in the dead of night.

When man lives in joy, he becomes like the sun: completely radiant in splendor and overpowering in strength. Joy is supernatural. It is the spirit of resurrection. It is the Transfiguration of Christ on Mount Tabor. It is St. Seraphim of Sarov enveloped in the Uncreated Light.[45] Why did Christ endure the Crucifixion? "For the *joy* that was set before Him [He] endured the cross, despising the shame, and has sat down at the right hand of the throne of God" (Heb. 12:2, emphasis added).

It could have been said, "For the *resurrection* set before Him, He endured the cross." What specifically was the joy that was set before the Suffering Servant? This is found in Isaiah: "He shall see [the fruit] of the labor of His soul, and be satisfied" (Is. 53:11). What is the fruit of the labor of His soul? Humanity and all of creation healed, redeemed, and restored. Christ was burning with the joy of heaven: the joy and victory of the kingdom of God making all things new.

The Spirit of Resurrection

There is an intimate connection between the joy of resurrection and the present reality of suffering. There is a spiritual correlation between the artist's ability to suffer like Christ and the joy he possesses in God. It is precisely because Christ was anointed with the oil of gladness that He was able to suffer for the life of the world.

Another poem:

God is the original rapture of man—hovering over the face
of the deep, burning with enthusiasm and desire over the genesis of creation—the original pulse of exaltation and ecstasy!
The Christ was able to suffer more than any other soul,
precisely because his soul was anointed with the oil of gladness! Only he, who knew the utter euphoria of heaven, could
endure the very flames of hell. Divine Love, wrapped in flesh
and blood, temperately pulsing with the uncorrupted expectancy of redemption. This very Christ is the naked Author
of Transcendence and the burning Creator of Awe—he looks
upon men, as they truly are—worthy of redeeming grace and
love, for he has never lost sight of their original virtue: a virtue which only the Suffering Christ could once again bestow.

The artist's ability to endure the tribulations of life is directly connected to the way she receives the joy of the Resurrection. Her intimacy with God directly determines in what fashion she will shine in the darkness of this world. Joy is the spirit of resurrection: because of the joy set before her, she can endure her cross.

THE SPIRIT OF DEFIANCE

The joy of the Lord is defiant toward evil. It does not give in. Even in the blackness of discouragement, joy lies in wait, anticipating the Sunday morning of the soul: the glorious vengeance of the Resurrection. Christ was so focused on the Resurrection that He "despised the shame," as it says in Hebrews. This is the spirit of defiance.

Our society seems to think that joy is a conflict-free, lucid state of contentment. It is not. It is an act of rebellion: a holy and sacred rage. It is one's choice finger lifted up in the face of the enemy. It is not placid, passive, or docile. It is the madness of love. It is the heavenly fire of Christ's Passion. For the joy set before Him, He endured the ultimate suffering.

One final poem:

This is my last act of defiance. This is my sacred rage, my holy madness. This is my soul's rebellion—to live in the radiance of your joy, and swim in the insanity of your bliss. This, my darling one, is our blessed vengeance upon the enemies of Love.

They shall not steal from this tower of devotion. They shall not prevail over this spirit of praise. I hold within my will the blade of divine joy, and I shall have my vengeance upon the minions of despair, which lurk behind every thought. Do you know, beloved, how they tremble to see us rise with the morning light?

Come with me, my dove, to a castle of ecstasy and longing, where both torch and shadow stand naked before us, fusing our spirits with solace and rage; the cold of the stone and the warmth of your body, moaning, in silent echoes of praise. With the wound of love pressed against our souls in hallowed fury. And the flame, the flame of the Presence between us, holding back the darkness from within, and the darkness from without.[46]

THE SPIRIT OF VENGEANCE

Joy is the artist's vengeance upon darkness. Many people today believe that the Light is soft and passive. From our culture's perspective, to become a Christian would be synonymous with getting neutered or spayed. I understand how this opinion has been reached. It is in response, not to the Christianity of the East, but to many misrepresentations and pendulum swings that mar the true Image of Christ in our culture.

Young people especially seem to think the darkness is intense, powerful, and rebellious. But in truth, the darkness is cowardly, insecure, and hopeless. The artist was made to rebel, but not against God—against evil. He was made to resist. The artist was created to be a courageous creature of consequence. If young people would only channel their rebellion against the darkness and their passion toward the Light, then creation would begin to see the sons and daughters of God revealed with power.

The Light is not soft or passive. Angels are not little babies with wings. They are mighty warriors who have already defeated the enemy of God and his army in heaven. Just look at the icons of Gabriel or Michael. Jesus Christ is the Lion of the tribe of Judah. He is the most fierce, defiant, and enigmatic warrior who ever lived. Indeed, He is the very Face of the Unseen God. His greatest desire is to restore the joy of Eden within man's heart.

The Joy of the Theotokos

When the Archangel Gabriel appeared to Mary the Theotokos to announce the miraculous conception of Christ, his first word was, "Rejoice!" The greeting "Hail Mary" means "Rejoice, Mary!" (Luke 1:28). And when the angelic host appeared to the shepherds the night Christ was born, they proclaimed, "Joy to the world!" (see Luke 2:10). This was not a passive choir, but an army of heavenly warriors. Both of these angelic visitations were proclamations of war against the darkness; and they came in the language of joy.

Joy is the very language of heaven.

There is a spiritual process of death and resurrection that plays out on a daily and seasonal basis in the realm of joy. The artist learns to rest in the Spirit, because the Spirit is the source of his joy. When Christ was baptized in the Jordan River, the Gospel says He was filled with the Holy Spirit and a voice from heaven spoke. Imagine that moment: "This is My Beloved Son, in whom I am well pleased" (Matt. 3:17). Talk about a high, right? This is the essence of heavenly joy: it doesn't get any better than this.

The next verse reads, "Then Jesus was led up by the Spirit into the wilderness to be tempted by the devil" (Matt. 4:1). Strange narrative on the surface. But this is an indication for the artist. There is a natural cycle of death and resurrection to the spiritual life. It is ultimately ineffective to try to circumvent this process. It is better to humbly follow the Spirit wherever He goes—even into the wilderness. At the appointed time, the artist will resurrect with the joy of paradise. There will be high moments of tangible grace, but it is useless to try to sustain these experiences in one's own strength, because the Spirit might be leading one into a desert. Besides, feelings are not the way the artist measures the presence of God in her life. Grace is given to her at Holy Baptism and it is within her, whether she feels it or not.

This process is not a punishment, nor is it vindictive. It is the natural manner of transformation. If the artist follows the Spirit, she will always be led to another resurrection. If Christ walks off the Mountain of Transfiguration, for instance, the artist must go with Him. The mountain no longer means anything if Christ is not on it. The manna goes bad when one attempts to store it (as the children of Israel discovered in the wilderness). The artist is taught to pray for her daily bread. This will keep her joy fresh and authentic if she allows the Spirit to lead and guide her into both cross and resurrection.

THE PARADOXICAL JOY OF WEAKNESS

For the spiritual artist, joy springs in its purest form from weakness, oftentimes amidst great sorrow. The ancient prophet declared, "The joy of the Lord is your strength" (Neh. 8:10). The word *strength* is synonymous with *power*, and this calls to mind another Scripture:

> And he [Christ] said to me, "My grace is sufficient for you, for My strength is made perfect in weakness." Therefore most gladly I will rather boast in my infirmities, that the power of Christ may rest upon me. Therefore I take pleasure in infirmities, in reproaches, in needs, in persecutions, in distresses, for Christ's sake. For when I am weak, then I am strong. (2 Cor. 12:9–10)

For the sake of this thesis, it could also be said this way: "My grace is sufficient for you, for My *joy* is made perfect in your weakness." His joy is our strength. Here we find a trinity of spiritual truth: grace is intimately connected to joy (as we discovered earlier) and joy is directly related to strength. Grace, joy, and strength: these three gifts of God are profoundly connected to the life of the artist.

Oftentimes, my preparation for scenes of great suffering has been tears of joy. Often, I would drive to work with thirty pages of heavy material memorized the night before, waiting to be performed—and for some reason tears of joy would fall from my face in praise to God. I found this to be very odd, and so I prayed and asked God why this was happening. The whisper in my heart was articulated, in essence, "I am filling you with the spirit of joy so that you will be able to suffer prophetically for the sake of others today."

For an artist, the worst inner state of existence would be numbness. Divine joy (the joy of Christ) counteracts the cancer of sloth and egoism. It keeps the artist alive and awake to both nature and God. Christ spoke passionately against humanity's instinct toward numbness: "You are neither cold nor hot. I could wish you were cold or hot. So then, because you are lukewarm, and neither cold nor hot, I will vomit you out of My mouth" (Rev. 3:15–16).

Strong language, indeed. Is He not trying to rouse humanity from the sleep of death? There are many things that will succeed in doing this, but suffering and joy are the most powerful. These paradoxical realities are radiantly displayed in the lives of the saints: there one discovers that suffering awakens man from his spiritual slumber and reawakens him to the spirit of joy.

Joy is the nourishment of the creative life.

Suffering keeps the artist awake within so that she is ready and available to rejoice with those who rejoice and weep with those who weep. This divine ecstasy is received through repentance, innocence, humility, weakness, and ultimately, mercy.

The first step is for the artist to embrace that she is utterly incapable, in her own strength, of living in the joy of paradise. The next step is for her to realize not only that she *is* weak, but also that she *gets* to be weak. It is a gift to let go and rest in the strength of God—not a burden.

Being weak does not mean lifeless, mechanical servitude, but freedom. The more the artist allows herself to be weak in the presence of God, the more she will experience supernatural joy. Therefore, weakness, as St. Paul wrote, is not something to shun, but something to boast about. Dependency is the key to the artist's joy and creative dynamism.

The artist is free only when he has limitations. As Peter Gabriel has noted, if you take away the boundaries, you castrate him. Creativity is born out of our limitations—in essence, our strength is discovered in our weakness. The power of Christ is made perfect in the artist's vulnerability. Only the weak can experience the supremacy of His love. "'Not by might nor by power, but by My Spirit,' / Says the Lord of hosts" (Zech. 4:6). This is the purest disposition of the human soul and the ultimate anthem of the artist.

The artist is a person of supernatural joy and strength. Everything he does on this earth comes from this place of rejoicing: this magnanimous union with God through the risen Christ. The joy of the resurrection floods the soul of the artist with mystical energy to inhabit the depths of humanity. When the artist embraces the mystery of God, the beauty of life increases and the madness of love abounds. Compassion floods the body, wisdom invades the senses, joy thrives within the spirit, and peace radiates within the heart. This prepares the artist to encounter the heart-wrenching beauty of the Divine and truly create in the Spirit.

Rejoice, O artists! Rejoice!

Lord Jesus Christ, Son of God,
have mercy on me, a sinner.

You, O Christ, are the fulfillment of every good thing.
Fill my soul with joy and gladness and save me,
for You alone are most merciful.

Epilogue

———◆———

QUESTIONS OF CHRIST AS THEY RELATE TO THE NATURE OF THE ARTIST

"Why is my character cutting you off in the middle of your speech? Should I really cross to the window at that moment? What's my character looking for in this scene? Why is he avoiding the truth? What's he afraid of? What does he want? What's the point of this scene? I'm not seeing it. Why? How come? What if? Do you have any ideas?"

This was only a fraction of the stream of questions I heaped on my trusted mentors when I was a child, just beginning my career. The whole process was one big inquiry, a discovery, a chance to grow and learn. I was a little human sponge, soaking up everything I could through observation, investigation, and osmosis. As I grew up, I began to realize that this instinctive impulse toward inquiry tends to wane. I would have to be intentional and disciplined to maintain the wonder and enthusiasm of a child.

Every work of art begins with questions. The artistic (and spiritual) journey consists of a continual return to innocence and simplicity. If an artist is writing a song, so many questions appear: "What is this song about? Who is the person behind the story? Is it coming from my own experience or someone else's? What is the soul of the song? Is it a question? A form of confession? Is it a song about revenge or resignation? Should I keep the verses short or allow a more in-depth portrait to be painted before the chorus?" All of these and more occur throughout the entire process. If an artist is writing a novel, it's the same foundation. Questions. Questions. Questions.

The Master of story, Jesus Christ, said, "Ask, and it will be given to you; seek, and you will find; knock, and it will be opened to you" (Matt. 7:7). In the spiritual life of the artist, it is just as important to ask the right questions as it is to have the right answers. Some questions (the artist discovers) have no answers: this is good and even necessary to draw closer to the mystery of God. Christ was constantly asking people questions. The nature of His questions is hauntingly significant for the artist.

THE FUNDAMENTAL QUESTION

"What do you seek?" (John 1:38)

The first question Christ asks in the Gospel of John is the most relevant question any artist could approach. It is also the cosmic question of mankind. The artist should revisit this question on a personal level often, because what he wants and what he is seeking directs the vessel of his soul amidst the untold storms of life. It also directs the creative vessel of the character he is portraying. This question is a creative compass for the artist. It is his way back to a clear and harmonious vision of who he is, who his fictional characters are, and what they most desire.

Christ asked people this question over and over throughout the Scriptures. It obviously carried great significance to the Son of God and the way He relates to us. He also repeatedly asked, "What do you want Me to do for you?" Jesus asked this of a blind man, and his response was this: "Lord, that I may receive my sight" (Luke 18:41). Is this not the condition of every human soul? Of every artist? Man is utterly blind to the mysterious grace and truth of Christ, and suddenly, at some unforeseen hour, the Messiah calmly asks, "What do you want Me to do for you?" The artist's daily response to this eternal question will establish the ultimate triumph or disillusionment of his soul.

If he remains within himself, so to speak, then he will simply trade one blindness for another, year after year. But if the artist reaches out to Christ, the Light of the World, then his blindness will continually be healed and restored.

It is essential that the poet call on Christ. But it is also important how or in what manner he calls on the Lord. The artist cries out to Christ for what he truly needs—things essential for his salvation: a new heart, a transformed mind, repentance, forgiveness, grace, humility, love, and peace. These are all descriptions of what the artist experiences when he receives the Holy Spirit. If he cries out for the Holy Spirit, the Spirit will be given to him. This is a certain "yes" from God. If, however, the artist asks for fame, notoriety, an extravagant car, or things of this kind, he obstructs the nature of prayer and reduces his relationship with God to a form of bartering.

"What do you want?" is the question burning at the center of the flame of heaven. It is always Christ who asks this question within the heart of man. It is always personal.

THE DILEMMA OF THE HUMAN HEART

"For what will it profit a man if he gains the whole world, and loses his own soul?" (Mark 8:36)

This question reveals the dilemma or condition of the human heart. Here humanity discovers a fearsome warning from the mouth of the Merciful One. Artists in particular are in great danger of falling into the delusion of vainglory. It is the original sin of Lucifer, who was the most splendid and radiant of angels. It was precisely his own beauty that he became enamored with—much like Narcissus, who fell in love with his own image (which is where the word *narcissist* comes from). Artists can very easily gain the admiration and applause of the world and lose their own soul by receiving its glory.

In the question above, we glimpse the absolute detachment Christ has toward the delusions of this world. He sees the drama of humanity not in the pale context of the temporal, but within the luminance of immortality. This sheds light on the destiny of the artist. It also gives him a unique vantage point from which to engage the plight of his fictional characters, songs, and stories. Creating a truly cosmic work of art requires this immanent spiritual and creative vision, at least subconsciously or instinctively. What is art, if not a fictional reflection of the actual drama taking place in the human heart?

Nicholas Berdyaev observes this metaphysical connection in his enlightening book, *Dostoevsky*:

> The denial of man's immortality is equivalent to a denial of man. Either he is an immortal spirit who carries an eternal destiny or else his is only an empirical and ephemeral phenomenon, the passive product of his natural and social surroundings. If the last be the case, he has no intrinsic value, and evil and sin do not exist. . . . If man is not a free, immortal, personal being he may do anything, he is responsible for nothing, he has no intrinsic value.[47]

These three things, which Berdyaev highlights, are essential ingredients to a faithful exposition of traditional Christian anthropology: man is *free*, *immortal*, and *personal*. Christ heightened both the moral demands and the romantic value of humankind by reminding man of his freedom, immortality, and personal uniqueness. Man is free to choose life or death; he has intrinsic, eternal value; and the Infinite God loves him personally. Receiving these truths makes it possible for man to return God's love to his fellow beings. It makes him capable of being human.

Christ came to write the law of God on man's heart. The precursor to Christ, the Mosaic Law, was given to mankind to awaken the conscience to the ever-fading memory of Eden, where there was no murder, stealing, lying, jealousy, or corruption of heart. But this Law was still written on tablets of stone. Christ fulfilled the Law's deepest intentions by mystically uniting us to God Himself. This synergistic relationship fulfills and transcends (not contradicts) the Law of Moses. In essence, Love (Christ) will do what the Law could not: remake men. Instead of merely undergoing behavior modification, man will literally be born again from the inside.

Christ revealed immortality as being personal and communal, not abstract or juridical. The memory of Eden was fully restored to the human heart with the advent of Christ and the Holy Spirit—not only the memory of what was, but also the hope of what is to come in the new Paradise.

This composite picture of the nature of man feeds the artist with an inexhaustible spiritual landscape to explore. It affects how he approaches every work of art and character he portrays or depicts. These fictional characters prophetically represent free, immortal, personal beings with longings and desires that transcend the mundane dreariness of this world—the purely psychological realities. Even if the character's awareness of these spiritual realities remains closed off (e.g., if he or she is an atheist), the access point remains the same for the artist.

This luminance of immortality places every piece of drama into its proper cosmic framework. This can be experienced only with the heart, imagination, and faith of a child.

By this question, Christ is showing man that even if he were to gain the entire world and all it has to offer, he would still suffer from a fearsome emptiness. He would still have a God-shaped hole within the core of his being. This enables the artist to possess a transcendent quality in every performance he gives and every work of art he creates. Christ is reorienting the values and desires of humanity. In essence He is saying, "You were made for love!" And not just any love, but the incorruptible love of God. This is where the artist finds his true humanity, in the embrace of eternal love.

A Question of Action

"But what do you think? A man had two sons,
and he came to the first and said, 'Son, go, work today
in my vineyard.' He answered and said, 'I will not,' but
afterward he regretted it and went. Then he came to the
second and said likewise. And he answered and said,
'I go, sir,' but he did not go. Which of the two did
the will of his father?" (Matt. 21:28–31)

This is a brilliant tutorial in the value of actions beyond mere words or dialogue. What a man does is more important than what he says. A person may say something for any number of reasons—but what is his or her subsequent action?

For instance, if the artist is portraying someone who commits adultery: The character may have said "I do" at his wedding—he may have even meant it at the time—but his ensuing actions of infidelity reveal the confusion and blindness of his heart. The character's actions reveal the power (or lack thereof) of his words. Christ understood this reality and emphasized its importance in the story mentioned above. The parable reveals two sons who display opposite contradictions. This confirms what we already know: Human beings are often confused about themselves. What they want to do and what they know they *ought* to do are often two different things.

The space between our words and our actions is the creative tension in which man abides. It is the arena of his moral universe. He lives and dies in this (often contradictory) space of free will. This is the Colosseum where he dons his various masks of concealment.

Man does not merely put on these masks for the sake of concealing himself from others. He also dons them for the sake of concealing himself from himself: his own fears and doubts. This is the true chaos man finds within himself. This is the hall of mirrors he so desperately wants to escape from— or does he? The Scriptures elsewhere confirm the supremacy of actions over hollow words: "For the kingdom of God *is* not in word but in power" (1 Cor. 4:20). Actions are powerful because they require the faith of the whole man. Anyone can talk about life: "I believe this" or "I love her." But what one actually believes and whom one truly loves is revealed by the resounding tone of one's actions.

For instance, anyone can preach forgiveness. It is quite another thing to live it while hanging from a cross, as Christ did for the life of the world. This is authentic forgiveness and love: the kind that cannot be discredited without some form of absurdity.

A QUESTION OF BEAUTY

"Did not He who made the outside make the inside also?" (Luke 11:40)

This question confirms the sacramental beauty of humanity. The artist does well to remember this union of the material and the spiritual world. The creative moment he is seeking to inhabit is found within and without. The ancient prayer to the Holy Spirit, "who is everywhere present and fills all things," guides him into unexpected moments of grace and creativity.

The holistic panorama the Trinity gives the artist is astounding. God is in his unseen thoughts and emotions, as well as the physical water he might be drinking or the glass he's holding in his hand. Christ is in the eyes of the other person as well as the trees surrounding him and the sky above. It is not only the Light that occupies both regions, but also the darkness, to varying degrees. This cosmic war is waged in both worlds: the spiritual and the material.

This question makes it clear that the original source of man and woman is God. It is He that made both the body and the spirit. He did not make the darkness that torments humanity, only the freedom to choose light or its opposite form. Therefore, the artist's ultimate and lasting freedom is found in the total embrace of his original source (the Person of God). This is where peace, healing, and authentic creativity are birthed.

A QUESTION OF INTIMACY

"Whom are you seeking?" (John 18:7)

This question is quite remarkable in its universal significance. The first question Christ asks in His public ministry is, "*What* do you want?" or "*What* are you seeking?" Then after His Resurrection, when Mary Magdalene is weeping beside the empty tomb, He asks, "Woman, why are you weeping? *Whom* are you seeking?" He has subtly and yet profoundly transitioned humanity from "what" to "whom do you want?"

Ultimately, man's truest desire is for a Person, not a state of being in isolation from Love. This question is at the core of every human heart. It is a prophetic picture of mankind. Man and woman weep beside the empty tomb of life and death, believing (or perhaps fearing) that God is dead—that He has abandoned them; or maybe He never cared about them in the first place. Adam and Eve are weeping within. Jesus Christ, having trampled down death by His death on the Cross and rising from the dead, stands before humanity and says, "Why are you weeping? Whom are you seeking?" (John 20:15).

It is fascinating that Mary could not recognize the risen Christ until He spoke her name, "Mary." At that moment, suddenly she could see (through her tear-filled eyes perhaps) the victorious Christ standing before her: the vanquisher of death. This inexpressible encounter is offered to every human being. But it is only when a person hears Christ speak his name that he is able to see the risen Lord for who He really is. Man's relationship with God is indeed personal—hauntingly so. It is not what man is seeking, but whom he is seeking, that matters in the end.

Along these lines, later in the same Gospel, Christ asks Peter three successive times, "Do you love Me?" (John 21:15–17). Why should this matter? Why would it matter to the infinite God? Why would the affection and fidelity of inconsequential, mortal creatures matter to the Transcendent God? Because God is Love, and man is made in His loving Image. The questions that lie at the heart of the universe are all ones of relationship and intimacy—not abstraction or philosophy.

There are so many more questions one could meditate on, but this book is not intended to be an exhaustive work on this specific subject. I would encourage the reader to seek more of the questions of Christ in the Scriptures. Contemplate them as they relate to you personally and as an artist. Ask boldly, search diligently, and pray earnestly for the truth, because in the end, it is only the Truth that sets one free. The life of the artist begins and ends with a Mystery.

"If you abide in My word, you are My disciples indeed. And you shall know the truth, and the truth shall make you free" (John 8:31–32).

Life of Saint Genesius of Rome

Genesius was a gifted actor, comedian, playwright, and the leader of a troupe of actors in Rome. When Diocletian initiated his great persecution, Genesius, who was a pagan, hatched a grand scheme to construct a play parodying the Christian Sacraments, to expose them to the ridicule of the audience.

Thus he resolved one day to represent Baptism, with all its ceremonies, as ludicrously as possible. To this effect he became well acquainted with all that takes place at Holy Baptism, appointed the parts for the play, and instructed the actors as to what they were to do.

On the day of the performance, Emperor Diocletian and his court were present. The comedy began, with Genesius acting the principal part. Feigning to be sick, he lay down, calling to his friends to bring him something to relieve his suffering. When they had done this, he said that he felt he was soon to die and wanted to become a Christian, and that they should "baptize" him. Everything was brought upon the stage that was used at baptism, and an actor playing a priest came on stage in order to "baptize" the ailing catechumen. All the questions were put to him that are put to those who are to be baptized. The ceremony was performed in so ludicrous a manner that the emperor and all the people shouted with laughter.

At the moment when the pagan actors scoffed and blasphemed the Holy Sacrament of the true Church, as the actor poured the water over his head, the Almighty touched the heart of Genesius and illumined it with a ray of His divine grace. As he saw the truth of Christianity, suddenly an entire change took place in the actor, and he loudly and earnestly proclaimed his faith in Jesus Christ.

His companions, not knowing what had happened, continued the blasphemous mockery. When the whole ceremony was performed, they threw a white robe over Genesius in derision of the garment usually given to the newly converted and baptized; thus clothed, they presented him to the people amidst great hilarity.

But Genesius, already a true believer in Christ, turned to the emperor and other spectators and confessed to them with great dignity what had taken place within him. He declared solemnly that until that day, blinded by idolatry, he had scoffed and derided Christianity, and therefore had proposed to represent baptism on the stage for the amusement of the people. But during the sacrilegious performance, his heart had suddenly changed, and he desired to become a Christian. He said he had seen the heavens open and perceived a hand that touched him when the baptismal water was poured over him. He further stated that before they had baptized him, he had seen an angel with a book in which all his past iniquities had been recorded, who assured him that they would all be washed away by Holy Baptism, and that he had in fact seen that all his vices had been obliterated from its pages. After relating this, he added that he renounced idolatry, and believing that Jesus Christ was the Son of God and the Redeemer of the world, he would henceforth live and die a Christian. In conclusion, he exhorted the emperor and all present to follow his example and worship the only true God.

It soon became clear to the emperor and the audience that Genesius was no longer acting. The emperor then became enraged at his noble and frank confession and gave immediate orders that his garments should be torn from him and that he should be whipped with scourges and clubs before all the people, and then be cast into prison. Plautian, the prefect, received orders to renew this punishment daily until Genesius would abandon his new faith and sacrifice to the pagan gods. The holy confessor was stretched upon the rack, torn with iron hooks, and burned with torches. As the prefect urged him to submit to the imperial command and sacrifice to the pagan gods, the holy martyr replied:

"Your emperor is but a mortal man; whoever desires the favor of such may seek it of him. I pray to the immortal King of heaven and earth, and will never forsake Him. I know that He who received me in Holy Baptism is the true King, and I repent for having so often derided and offended Him. I will not obey Diocletian, whose reign will soon be over, and who will one day become as naught. You may torture me, therefore, as much as you like; I will remain faithful to my God. If you had the power to kill me a hundred times, you would not be able to take Him out of my heart or my mouth."

Plautian, provoked at Genesius's fearlessness, reported his words to the emperor, who ordered him beheaded, which sentence was executed in year of our Lord 303. Thus St. Genesius, who from an idolater became a Christian, and from a scoffer of Christianity a fearless confessor of the Savior, received the crown of martyrdom.

Hearing of his death, the Christians realized Genesius had been converted and put to death for the faith. They managed to secure his body and buried him in the Cemetery of St. Hippolytus on the Via Tiburtina with other Christian martyrs. When the persecution ended and following the Christianization of Rome, his remains were exhumed and later solemnly enshrined in the Church of San Giovanni della Pigna near the Pantheon in Rome.

The church at Rome that was dedicated in his honor from ancient times was restored and beautified by Gregory III in 741. In 1591 his relics were transferred to a tomb in the Church of Santa Susanna, where they lie to this day.

Since early times Genesius has been considered the patron saint of actors, actresses, comedians, and those who work in the theatrical arts; with the advent of cinema, he is also regarded as its patron. More recently he has also been adopted as a patron of converts, dancers, and epileptics.[48]

Saint Genesius of Rome, pray for us.

Acknowledgments

I am eternally indebted to my wife, Elisa, the love of my life: for your selfless heart, your faithful devotion to Christ, the Lover of your soul, and the innumerable ways in which you have inspired me to always pursue the light. *Cara mia, ti amo.* All three of my children: Caleb, you are so full of goodness, love, and wisdom. You feel things deeply and live with a purity of heart that I long to emulate. Thank you for being a warrior for Divine Love. Adora, you are truly beloved, as your name reveals. You are filled with the innocence of heaven and the fire of the resurrection. Thank you for loving your daddy so much and always believing in me—I treasure you, little angel. Titus, you have the strength of the kingdom in you. You are so radiant with the joy of being loved and loving the world around you. Thank you for your smiles, hugs, and kisses—they uplift your daddy's heart every day.

To my amazing parents, Rick and Jeanine: Thank you for every sacrifice of love you have made on my behalf, both seen and unseen. Your unconditional love has provided the freedom to explore the depths of truth without fear. My brother Richard and your family: Your friendship is an invaluable gift in my life. Thank you for listening to the insanity of transformation and growth without judgment. I hope to live with half as much humility and grace as you. My sister Candice: What a journey we have had together—thank you for your uncompromising love and compassion for my family and myself. I am in awe of who you are, and I am inexpressibly grateful for your friendship and love.

Anthony Geary, this book would not exist without the humility of your heart and guidance over the years. You took an eleven-year-old boy and gave him the respect of a veteran and the love of a son. You are not only one of the best actors who ever lived, but also one of the most amazing individuals I have ever known. You teach by example the often-neglected virtue of humility in the life of the actor. We have soared to rare heights together that one could only describe as transcendent. Thank you for your friendship and inexhaustible love for me. You are with me in every scene I do. Love you.

Richard Brander, thank you for your encouragement and wisdom. You planted some very good seeds in the heart of this young student.

To every artist who has left an indelible mark on my heart: Thank you for the honor of working with you and sharing the unrepeated moment of creation with you. Graciella Sanchez, for your vision, dedication, and belief in me. Leon Gladstone and Meg Thayer, you continue to inspire me.

Msgr. Jim Lisante, for your deep love, affection, and generosity. Your friendship means so much to me and to my family as well. I am so grateful to walk this road with you.

Fr. Andrew Stephen Damick: Thank you for offering to interview me for your blog on Ancient Faith Radio. Little did I know a friendship would be sparked that has meant so much.

Everyone at Holy Virgin Mary Cathedral, for welcoming us into the embrace of the Holy Orthodox Church. Fr. John Strickland, Matushka Yelena, and your precious children: Thank you for your wisdom, prayers, and teachings. The humility and joy of Christ and His Resurrection are so present in your lives. My family and I are forever thankful for your faithfulness to the Lover of mankind. We love you!

My godfather Gary Hart: Our coffee times together have been crucial, edifying, and enjoyable. Fr. Stephen Rogers and everyone at St. Ignatius: You have welcomed us into your hearts, and your devotion to the Holy Trinity is palpable. Thank you!

Monk Gregory, for your prayers and gentle boldness. My heart is enriched by our friendship. Metropolitan Jonah and Father Damascene for your wisdom, graciousness, and humility. Geronda Alexios, Father Jeremiah, and all the monks of the Holy Monastery of Xenophontos on Mount Athos, for your prayers and inspiration. Geronda Ephraim, Father Theonas, Father Andrew, and all the brotherhood of the Holy Monastery of Vatopaidi, for your prayers, love, and support.

John Maddex, Katherine Hyde, Matt Dorning, and everyone at Ancient Faith Publishing, for guiding this book to publication. Thank you for your belief in this project, and your work and wisdom in improving it!

Finally, thank you to everyone who posted comments on YouTube and sent encouraging emails after the Emmys in

June of 2012. My wife and I were deeply moved and humbled to experience the joy and prayers of so many Orthodox Christians around the world. Many years!

Additional Questions of Christ for Prayer and Meditation

THE GOSPEL ACCORDING TO MATTHEW

"For if you love those who love you, what reward have you?" (5:46)

"Is not life more than food and the body more than clothing?" (6:25)

"Which of you by worrying can add one cubit to his stature?" (6:27)

"And why do you look at the speck in your brother's eye, but do not consider the plank in your own eye?" (7:3)

"Do you believe that I am able to do this?" (9:28)

"Have you understood all these things?" (13:51)

"What will a man give in exchange for his soul?" (16:26)

"Should you not also have had compassion on your fellow servant, just as I had pity on you?" (18:33)

"What do you think about the Christ? Whose Son is He?" (22:42)

"My God, My God, why have You forsaken Me?" (27:46)

THE GOSPEL ACCORDING TO MARK

"Why do *you* reason about these things in your hearts?" (2:8)

"Why are you so fearful? How is it that you have no faith?" (4:40)

"Is it not written, 'My house shall be called a house of prayer for all nations'?" (11:17)

"Why do you test Me?" (12:15)

THE GOSPEL ACCORDING TO LUKE

"Can the blind lead the blind? Will they not both fall into the ditch?" (6:39)

"But why do you call Me 'Lord, Lord,' and not do the things which I say?" (6:46)

"Where is your faith?" (8:25)

"What is your name?" (8:30)

"Who do the crowds say that I am?" (9:18)

"But who do you say that I am?" (9:20)

"What is the kingdom of God like? And to what shall I compare it?" (13:18)

"Why do you sleep?" (22:46)

"Why are you troubled? And why do doubts arise in your hearts?" (24:38)

THE GOSPEL ACCORDING TO JOHN

"If I have told you earthly things and you do not believe, how will you believe if I tell you heavenly things?" (3:12)

"Do you want to be made well?" (5:6)

"How can you believe, who receive honor from one another, and do not seek the honor that comes from the only God?" (5:44)

"If I tell the truth, why do you not believe Me?" (8:46)

"Did I not say to you that if you would believe you would see the glory of God?" (11:40)

"Do you know what I have done to you?" (13:12)

"Will you lay down your life for My sake?" (13:38)

"Do you not believe that I am in the Father, and the Father in Me?" (14:10)

"Do you now believe?" (16:31)

"Are you speaking for yourself about this, or did others tell you this concerning Me?" (18:34)

Suggested Reading

Alexander Schmemann, *For the Life of the World* (Crestwood, NY: St. Vladimir Seminary Press, 1973)

Paul Evdikomov, *The Art of the Icon: A Theology of Beauty* (Redondo Beach, CA: Oakwood Publications, 1990)

Archimandrite Aimilianos of Simonopetra, *The Way of the Spirit: Reflections on Life in God* (Greece: Indeiktos, 2009)

Nicholas Berdyaev, *Dostoevsky* (New York: Meridian Books, 1957)

Kyriacos C. Markides, *The Mountain of Silence: A Search for Orthodox Spirituality* (New York: Image Publishing, 2002)

Paul Evdokimov, *In the World of the Church* (Crestwood, NY: St. Vladimir Seminary Press, 2000)

Elder Porphyrios, *Wounded by Love* (Limni, Evia, Greece: Denise Harvey, 2005)

Fyodor Dostoevsky, *The Brothers Karamazov*

Leonard Cohen, *Book of Mercy* (Toronto, Ontario: McClelland & Stewart, 1984)

—⊰◈⊱—

Endnotes

1   Elder Porphyrios, *Wounded by Love*, John Raffan, trans. (Limni, Evia, Greece: Denise Harvey, 2005) http://www.goodreads.com/quotes/196072-whoever-wants-to-become-a-christian-must-first-become-a

2   Lewis, C. S., *An Experiment in Criticism* (Cambridge University Press, 1961), p. 19

3   Schmemann, Alexander, *The Eucharist* (Crestwood, NY: St. Vladimir's Seminary Press, 1988), p. 20

4   This quotation, derived from Dostoevsky's novel *The Idiot*, is actually a statement attributed to the main character, Prince Myshkin, in the form of a question from another character: "Is it true, prince, that you said once that 'beauty' would save the world?"

5   Dostoevsky, Fyodor, *The Brothers Karamazov*, Constance Garnett, trans. (New York: Barnes & Noble Inc., 1995)

6   Protopresbyter Gregory Petrov, *The Akathist Hymn*, Glory to God for All Things.

7   Plato, *The Republic* (Dover Publications, 2000). Plato attributes this quote to Damon of Athens.

8   The Service of Holy Baptism, Greek Orthodox Archdiocese, http://www.goarch.org/chapel/liturgical_texts/baptism

9   Van Gogh, Vincent, *Van Gogh on Art and Artists: Letters to Emile Bernard* (Dover Publications, 2003), p. 45

10 Tarkovsky, Andrei, *A Poet in the Cinema*, documentary (1983) https://www.youtube.com/watch?v=PTvIybrtMqU

11 Michael Stipe being interviewed by Charlie Rose, date unknown; https://www.youtube.com/watch?v=oLoI-JCQg7s

12 *Ostrov* (*The Island*), 2006, NTSC version with English subtitles

13 Saint John Climacus, *The Ladder of Divine Ascent* (Brookline, MA, Holy Transfiguration Monastery, 2012), Step 30, Paragraph 3, p. 244

14 Saint John Chrysostom, Catherine P. Roth and David Anderson, trans., *On Marriage and Family Life* (Crestwood, NY: St. Vladimir Seminary Press, 1986), p. 71

15 Jackson, J. S. (Jonathan), *Book of Solace and Madness* (Battle Ground, WA: Hilasterion Publishing, 2012)

16 Schmemann, Alexander, *For the Life of the World* (Crestwood, NY: St. Vladimir Seminary Press, 1973), p. 16

17 Evdokimov, Paul, *In the World, of the Church* (Crestwood, NY: St. Vladimir Seminary Press, 2000), p. 201

18 Muse, Stephen, *When Hearts Become Flame* (Rollinsford, NH: Orthodox Research Institute, 2011), p. 18

19 Saint John Climacus, *The Ladder of Divine Ascent*, quoted in Norris J. Chumley, *The Mysteries of the Jesus Prayer* (New York: HarperCollins and HarperOne, 2011), p. 54

20 Benedicta Ward, trans., *The Sayings of the Desert Fathers* (Kalamazoo, MI: Cistercian Publications, 1984). Here is the excerpt: "Abba Lot went to see Abba Joseph and said to him, 'Abba, as far as I can I say my little office, I fast a little, I pray and meditate, I live in peace and as far as I can, I purify my thoughts. What else can I do?' Then the old man stood up and stretched his hands towards heaven. His fingers became like ten lamps of fire and he said to him, 'If you will, you can become all flame.'" (p. 103)

21 Fellini, Federico, http://www.goodreads.com/quotes/tag/silence?page=2

22 Saint Ignatius of Antioch, AD 67–107, *The Epistle to the Ephesians* (Penguin Classics, 1987), p. 65

23 His All Holiness Ecumenical Patriarch Bartholomew, *Encountering the Mystery: Understanding Orthodox Christianity Today* (New York: Doubleday, 2008), p. 209

24 Patriarch Bartholomew, *op. cit.*, p. 208

25 http://www.byzcath.org/index.php/about-us-mainmenu-60/3-from-the-church-fathers/from-the-church-fathers/114-st-john-of-kronstadt-my-life-in-christ

26 Muse, *op. cit.*, p. 49

27 Hopko, Fr. Thomas, podcast *Creativity and Art (Part 1)*, August 2006, http://www.ancientfaith.com/specials/hopko_lectures

28 http://www.goodreads.com/author/quotes/182763.Michelangelo

29 Petrov, *op. cit.*

30 Evdokimov, *op. cit.*, p. 210

31 Patriarch Jeremiah II of Constantinople, quoted in George Mastrantonis, *Augsburg and Constantinople* (Brookline, MA: Holy Cross Orthodox Press, 1982), p. 35

32 Archimandrite Aimilianos of Simonopetra, *The Way of the Spirit* (Greece: Indeiktos, 2009)

33 Quoted in Chumley, *op. cit.*, p. 57

34 Ibid.

35 Lewis, C. S., *An Experiment in Criticism* (Cambridge University Press, 1961), pp. 140, 141

36 Elder Porphyrios, op. cit.

37 http://orthodoxwiki.org/Isaac_of_Syria

38 Markides, Kyriacos C., *The Mountain of Silence* (New York: Image Publishing, 2002), p. 77

39 Muse, *op. cit.*, p. 16

40 Hopko, Fr. Thomas, podcast cited above. Fr. Hopko quotes *The Arena* by Saint Ignatius Brianchaninov to elaborate his point.

41 Ibid.

42 Archimandrite Aimilianos of Simonopetra, *op. cit.*

43 Ibid.

44 Lewis, C. S., *Letters to Malcolm, Chiefly on Prayer* (Mariner Books, 2002), p. 93

45 See Saint Seraphim of Sarov, *On the Acquisition of the Holy Spirit*

46 Jackson, J. S. (Jonathan), *op. cit.*

47 Berdyaev, Nicholas, *Dostoevsky* (New York: Meridian Books, 1957)

48 This Life of Saint Genesius is adapted from http://orthodoxwiki.org/Genesius_of_Rome

About the Author

Jonathan Jackson began his career in Hollywood over twenty years ago on the soap opera *General Hospital*. His heart-wrenching performances helped win him five Emmy Awards. Jonathan has also performed in many feature films, including *The Deep End of the Ocean*, *Tuck Everlasting*, and *Insomnia*. His work has taken him to many places around the world, including Ireland, Italy, Romania, and Canada.

Jonathan is currently one of the stars of the ABC prime-time drama *Nashville*, a show centered on the inner workings of the Nashville music scene. He plays Avery Barkley, an up-and-coming singer/songwriter trying to find his way in Music City.

Along with acting, Jonathan is also the lead singer of the band Enation and the author of *Book of Solace and Madness*, which was published in 2012. Jonathan resides in Nashville, Tennessee, where he loves spending time with his wife, Elisa, and their three children.

For more, visit www.JonathanJackson.com

Ancient Faith Publishing hopes you have enjoyed and benefited from this book. The proceeds from the sales of our books only partially cover the costs of operating our nonprofit ministry—which includes both the work of **Ancient Faith Publishing** and the work of **Ancient Faith Radio.** Your financial support makes it possible to continue this ministry both in print and online. Donations are tax-deductible and can be made at www.ancientfaith.com.

To view our other publications,
log onto our website: **store.ancientfaith.com**

ANCIENT FAITH RADIO

Bringing you Orthodox Christian music, readings, prayers,
teaching, and podcasts 24 hours a day since 2004 at
www.ancientfaith.com